Praise for *One Good Turn*:

'A diverting testament to human ingenuity and a considerable feat of research, *One Good Turn*... will doubtless provide considerable pleasure to the armchair DIY enthusiast'
The Times on Sunday

'A sensual little book...as authentic and tactile as its contents'
Daily Express

'Next time you take a plane, don't try to stretch out the less interesting parts of a newspaper. Read this book and feel refreshed and enriched. You'll feel the benefit the next time you visit a museum and find yourself seeing everything in a new way'
New Scientist

'In his absorbing and instructive history of the screwdriver, Rybczynski frequently digresses to offer engaging mini-biographies of some of the mechanical geniuses behind seemingly simple tools'
Boston Herald

Also by Witold Rybczynski

ONE GOOD TURN

A Natural History of the Screwdriver and the Screw

WITOLD RYBCZYNSKI

Scribner

First published in Great Britain by Simon & Schuster, 2000
This edition first published by Scribner, 2001
An imprint of Simon & Schuster UK Ltd
A Viacom Company

1 3 5 7 9 10 8 6 4 2

Simon & Schuster UK Ltd
Africa House
64 -78 Kingsway
London WC2B 6AH

Simon & Schuster Australia
Sydney

A CIP catalogue record for this book is available from
the British Library

ISBN 0-7432-0850-1

Printed and bound in Great Britain by Omnia Books Ltd, Glasgow *to Shirley*

CONTENTS

Heurēka! [I've found it!]

—ARCHIMEDES

ONE GOOD TURN

CHAPTER ONE

The Carpenter's Toolbox

THIS ALL STARTS with a telephone call from David Shipley, an editor at the *New York Times*. Would I write an article for a special millennium issue of the Sunday magazine? he asks. The end of the millennium is on many magazine editors' minds, and I have had a number of such requests. Shipley explains that the theme of the issue is The Best of the Millennium. That sounds interesting. "What do you want me to write about?" I ask.

"We're hoping that you can write a short essay about the best tool," he answers.

I am a bit let down. *The best tool* is hardly as weighty a subject as *the best architect* or *the best city,* topics I could really sink my teeth into. Still, I have been working on a long biography and would welcome a break. Writing about the best tool of the millennium might even be fun.

While David Shipley is speaking, I compose the essay in my head. There is so much to choose from: paper clips, fountain pens, eyeglasses. I have recently seen a portrait in the Pennsylvania Academy of the Fine Arts of Benjamin Franklin wearing round spectacles, a reminder that Franklin was the inventor of the bifocal. Yet eyeglasses are much older than the eighteenth century. The first reference to eyeglasses is in a sermon given by a Dominican friar in Florence in 1306. He mentions that eyeglasses were invented twenty years earlier, and that he has even spoken with the inventor, although he neglects to give his name.[1] Medieval eyeglasses were only for farsighted people and were used for reading and writing. They were the first practical application of the new science of optics, paving the way for such far-reaching inventions as the telescope and the microscope. A key influence on literacy, astronomy, and biology, eyeglasses surely qualify as "the best tool of the millennium." This is going to be easy.

However, when I mention my idea to David, it becomes clear that he has something else in mind. He means *tool* in the literal sense—a handsaw or a hammer. So, not eyeglasses. He must hear the disappointment in my voice, and he points out that I once wrote a book about building my own house. That might make a good starting point, he suggests helpfully. All right, I say, I'll think about it.

In my case, "building my own house" meant actually building it. My wife and I, with the occasional help of friends, mixed concrete, sawed wood, plastered walls, and installed plumbing. We did everything ourselves except the electrical wiring. Ever since my boyhood experiences with recalcitrant train sets, I have been thwarted by electricity. Despite my father's patient explanations—he was an electrical engineer—and a college physics course, I never grasped the relationship between voltage, current, and resistance. Electricity, in fact, was a problem in our house-building project—there was none. We were building on a rural site about eight hundred feet from the road, and although we planned to bring in power, initially we could not afford the cost of a temporary line. Renting a gas-powered generator would be expensive, too—and noisy. I decided to build the framing and exterior of the house by hand. Once the basic structure was finished, which promised to take a year or two, we would bring in a line and hire a professional to install the electrical wiring.

Does one of my carpenter's tools qualify as the millennium's best? I discount power tools. I had used a portable circular saw, a drill, and a sander for finishing and cabinetwork, but these are chiefly laborsaving devices. Not that productivity isn't important. Ken Kern, the author of *The Owner-Built Home,* estimates that cutting all the two-by-fours for the frame of a small house would take seven full days using a handsaw, and only thirty minutes using a power saw.[2] I appreciate the ease of cutting wood with power tools, but the result, while more quickly arrived at, is no different than if I use a handsaw. In any case, I enjoy working with my hands. One of the rewards of building something yourself—a house or a bookshelf—is the pleasure of using tools. Hand tools are true extensions of the human body, for they have evolved over centuries of trial and error. Power tools are more convenient, of course, but they lack precisely that sense of refinement. No doubt, if I spent my life hammering nails, I would feel differently about the virtues of a nail gun, say. Yet increasing the productivity of carpenters does not seem to me in the same category as the invention of entirely new devices such as eyeglasses.

That leaves my box of hand tools. The tools required for the construction of a small wood-frame house fall roughly into four categories: measurement, cutting and shaping, hammering, and drilling. My measuring tools include a try square, a bevel, a chalk line, a plumb bob, a spirit level, and a tape measure. A little reading informs me that almost all these tools predate our millennium; indeed, most predate the *first* millennium of the Christian age. A Roman builder, or *mensor aedificorum,* was familiar with the try square, the plumb line, and the chalk line—all tools that were developed by the anc ient Egyptians.[3] The level, or *libella,* also an Egyptian invention, consisted of a wood frame resembling the letter A, with a plumb bob suspended from the apex. To level, the string was lined up with a mark in the center of the crossbar. Not as compact as my spirit level, perhaps, but obviously just as serviceable since A-levels continued to be used until the mid-1800s. The spirit level, with its sealed tube containing an air bubble floating in alcohol, was invented in the mid-1600s. It was first exclusively a surveying instrument—it took another two hundred years to find its way into the carpenter's toolbox. For measuring length, the Roman *mensor* used a *regula*, or a wooden stick divided into feet, palms, twelfths or *unciae* (whence our inches), and *digiti* or finger widths. I have a yardstick, too, but most of my measuring is done with a retractable steel tape. That, at least, would impress my Roman counterpart, whose only compact measuring device was a one-foot bronze folding rule. Oak yardsticks were used in the Middle Ages, and folding rules, in ivory, brass, or boxwood, reappeared in the eighteenth century. I can't find the origins of the tape measure, but I would guess that it was developed sometime in the late 1800s. I would be lost without my twenty-five-foot retractable tape measure, but it does not seem to me to qualify as the best tool of the millennium.

I own several saws. The handsaw, too, is an ancient tool: archaeologists have found metal-toothed Egyptian saws dating back to 1500 B.C. They have broad blades, some as long as twenty inches, curved wooden handles, and irregular teeth. The blades are copper, a soft metal. To keep the blade from buckling, the Egyptian saw was pulled—not pushed. Pulling is less effective than pushing, since the carpenter cannot bear down on the cutting stroke, and sawing wood must have been a slow and laborious process.* The Romans made two important improvements. They used iron for the blades, which made them stiffer, and they set the teeth of the saw to project alternatively right and left, which had the effect of making the saw-cut—or kerf—slightly wider than the blade, allowing smooth movement.

The Romans also invented the stiffened backsaw, whose blade is reinforced at the top. This prevents straight-through cuts, but the tool is useful for cabinetwork, especially when used in combination with a miter box. The most ingenious Roman addition to cutting tools is the frame saw. A relatively inexpensive narrow blade is held in a wooden frame and is kept taut by tightening a cord. Wooden frame saws worked so well that they remained the most common type of saw well into the nineteenth century (the principle of the frame saw survives in the modern hacksaw). In the mid–seventeenth century, a new type of saw was introduced in Holland

---

*Traditional Japanese saws likewise are pulled rather than pushed. With paper-thin blades, they are used chiefly for delicate cabinetwork.

and England. It had a broad, unstayed blade and a wooden pistol-grip handle. The rigid blade, originally made by rolling steel strips, makes a more accurate cut than a frame saw, and there is no frame to interfere with deep cuts. This effective tool became the basic modern handsaw. My workhorse is a twenty-six-inch Disston crosscut handsaw, with a skew-back blade, first introduced in 1874 by Henry Disston, a Philadelphia sawmaker. The open handsaw is a definite contender for best tool, but while it is certainly an elegant solution to an old problem, I think that David expects something a little more momentous.

The chief shaping device of the carpenter is the plane. The box plane is nothing more than a holder for a chisel blade, but it marks an important moment in the evolution of hand tools. Unlike an adze or a chisel, which depend on the skill of the craftsman, the effectiveness of a plane is built-in; that is, the carpenter does not need to control the blade, he provides only the motive force. One historian has called the plane "the most important advance in the history of woodworking tools."[4] That makes it sound like a worthy candidate for best tool of the millennium. Unfortunately, I find that the plane, too, is a Roman invention.

Chisels have more ancient origins. Bronze Age carpenters used chisels with both integral handles and socketed wooden handles in house and furniture construction. The first mallets, which resembled bowling pins, were pounded across the grain and had a short working life. Eventually, a handle was fitted to a separate head, whose harder end-grain made a more durable hammering surface. Heavy, long-handled mallets are called mauls. Eighteenth-century carpenters used a huge maul, known as the Commander, to drive together the joints of timber-framed houses and barns. The Commander has a head six inches in diameter and a foot long. I didn't have anything that big, but I did use a steel sledgehammer to coax stubborn joists and studs into place.

The most unusual hammer I own comes from a hardware market in Mexico City. Made in China, it is a "combination case opener," that is, a packing-crate opener. Like the specialized shingler's hammer, which combines a hammer and a hatchet, the case opener incorporates several tools: a hammer, a nail puller, a hatchet, and a crowbar. Mine must have been made in one of Mao's backyard furnaces, for shortly after I bought it, one of the metal claws broke off as I was pulling nails. Nevertheless, I still have it. While I am unsentimental about most possessions, I have never thrown away a tool.

I have always thought of combination tools as particularly modern gadgets—I am embarrassed to recollect that I once gave my father a screwdriver with a built-in flashlight as a Christmas present. In fact, the combination tool is ancient. The two oldest woodworking tools are the ax, for felling trees, and the adze—with its blade turned ninety degrees—used for dressing timber. A combination ax-adze was used by the Minoan civilization of Crete, which also invented the double-headed ax. The ax-adze was popular with Roman carpenters. The Romans, who invented forged iron nails, used another dual-purpose tool: the claw hammer. Pulling nails exerts heavy pressure on the handle, which risks being pulled out of its socket, or eye. Medieval English claw hammers sometimes had two metal straps that reinforced the connection to the handle. An American was responsible for the modern form of the claw hammer. In 1840, a Connecticut blacksmith, inspired by the adze, added a tapered neck that extended down the hammer handle, resulting in the so-called adze-eye hammer, which survives to this day.

Ancient Egyptian woodworkers used wooden pegs instead of nails. They made the holes with a bow drill. The bow drill, probably adapted from a fire-stick, has a cord wrapped around the drill and held taut by a bow. Holding the drill vertically, the carpenter moves the bow back and forth, like a cellist, pressing down on alternate turns. Because the carpenter exerts downward pressure with only one hand—and the cord can easily slip—the bow drill is ineffective for heavy drilling. (Bow drills continued to be used for delicate drilling until the nineteenth century.) Moreover, since each drilling stroke is followed by an idle return stroke, the bow drill wastes energy. Once again, it was the Romans who found a solution: the auger. The auger has a short wooden cross-handle, attached to a steel shaft whose tip is a spoon-shaped bit. The carpenter, holding the handle with both hands, can apply both great rotational force and heavy downward pressure. A particular variation of the auger, developed in the Middle Ages for drilling deep holes in ships' timbers, is called a breast auger. It is topped by a

A medieval workman with his tools, including a carpenter's brace. Detail from *Bearing the Cross*, part of an altarpiece painted by Meister Franke, 1424.

broad pad on which the carpenter rested the entire weight of his body.

The auger is a great advance, but it has one drawback: the bit tends to freeze in the wood between turns. The great breakthrough in drilling tools occurred during the Middle Ages with the invention of the carpenter's brace. The brace holds the same spoon-shaped bits as an auger, but the handle is shaped in such a way that it is possible—for the first time in history—to drill holes with a continuous rotation. A rounded pad atop the brace enables the carpenter to push down on the bit as he turns with a smooth back-and-forth motion.

One of the earliest representations of a brace is contained in the right-hand panel of an altar triptych painted about 1425 by the Flemish artist Robert Campin and now hanging in the Metropolitan Museum of Art in New York. The subject is Saint Joseph in his workshop. Joseph is making mousetraps (this is an allegorical painting), and he is surrounded by tools—a hammer and nails, a chisel, pincers, a straight saw, and an auger. He is holding a carpenter's brace and is drilling a hole in a piece of wood that he awkwardly balances on the arm of his chair.

What is striking about the tool that Joseph is holding is that it is identical to the eighteenth-century wooden braces I have seen in collections of American tools, and basically not much different from the brace in my own toolbox (although mine is steel). Some tools, such as hammers and saws, evolve slowly over centuries; others, such as planes, seemingly spring to life fully formed. The brace seems to have been such a case—it bears no resemblance to the auger or the bow drill. The brace has no antecedents because it incorporates an entirely new scientific principle: the crank. The crank is a mechanical device with a unique characteristic: it changes reciprocal motion—the carpenter's arm, moving back and forth—into rotary motion—the turning bit. The historian Lynn White Jr. characterized the discovery of the crank as "second in importance only to the wheel itself."[5] The crank made possible not only the carpenter's brace, but also hand-cranked mills and grinders, as well as a variety of water- and wind-driven machines such as stamping mills and pumps, and eventually steam engines.

There is no material or textual evidence that the crank existed in antiquity—as far as we know, it is a medieval European discovery.[6] The oldest representation of a crank is in a fourteenth-century medieval treatise that shows a design for a boat with a manual crank drive that resembles the kind of recreational foot-driven paddleboat that is a staple of summer-cottage lakes and city parks.[7] A Bavarian book on military engineering published in 1405 includes a sketch of a milling machine turned by a hand crank.[8] At about the same time, cranked lecterns (similar to modern dentists' adjustable tables) were used by scholars to swing books within convenient reading range.[9] So, around 1400, cranks were in the air. Whether the carpenter's brace came first or was inspired by one of these other gadgets, there is no doubt that this simple tool was the first practical application of the crank on a broad scale. The origin of the name *brace*, incidentally, is obscure. The tool was first called a piercer, for it was used to drill starting holes that were then enlarged with an auger. One historian speculates that *brace* may refer to the metal braces that were sometimes added to reinforce the crank shape.[10]

The carpenter's brace is a good tool and it definitely belongs to our millennium. But, as far as my essay is concerned, there is a problem: the brace is, well, boring. Despite the importance of the crank, the carpenter's brace itself never really developed further. The only nonwoodworking application occurred in the sixteenth century, when surgical braces, called trephines, were used to cut out a disk of bone from the skull. Otherwise, the brace seems to have had an uneventful history. It was merely a better way of drilling holes.

I have spent a week thinking and reading without making much progress. Since I am embarrassed to admit to David Shipley that I can't come up with a subject, it's beginning to look as if I will have to write about the unexciting carpenter's brace. This is not going to be an easy assignment; what had seemed like fun is turning into a chore. Dejected, I mention my predicament to my wife, Shirley. She thinks for a moment and answers, "There is one tool that I've always had at home. A screwdriver." I look at her skeptically. "Definitely, a screwdriver," she says. "Wherever I've lived, I've always had a screwdriver in the kitchen drawer. Preferably the kind that has several interchangeable heads, or whatever those end pieces are called." She adds conclusively, "You always need a screwdriver for something."

I had forgotten the screwdriver. I go back to my standard reference on hand tools, William Louis Goodman's *History of Woodworking Tools*, published in 1964. Goodman was a thirty-year veteran of teaching wood shop in an English boys' school. He was also a tool collector. I have the impression that he was someone who not only knew a lot about the origin of the Saxon adze, but could also give a handy personal demonstration of its proper use.

I look up *screwdriver* in Goodman's index—nothing. That's odd. Flipping through the book, I find an entire chapter on the carpenter's bench, a meditation on the origin of the glue pot, but nothing about screwdrivers. Then a chart catches my eye: "Woodworkers' Tool Kits at Various Periods."[11] It lists the times when various carpentry tools were invented and confirms what I already know—most hand tools originated during the Roman period. The Middle Ages added the carpenter's brace; the Renaissance, some specialized planes. The next period, "1600 to 1800," saw the invention of the spoke-shave, a sort of pulling knife used to make wheel spokes and chair spindles. Finally, in "1800 to 1962," I find the screwdriver. It is one of the last additions to the wood-worker's toolbox.

Usually, my 1949 edition of the *Encyclopaedia Britannica* is informative, but the entry "Screwdriver" is a simple definition—no history. The "Tools" entry does not even mention screwdrivers. I check the on-line *Britannica*, which is more helpful: "The handled screwdriver is shown on the woodworker's bench after 1800 and appears in inventories of tool kits from that date."[12] At least it isn't another Roman invention. I'm not convinced that the screwdriver is any more earthshaking than the carpenter's brace, and it is a laughably simple tool. Still, I am puzzled by its late appearance. It is definitely worth looking into.

CHAPTER TWO

Turnscrews

I START MY SEARCH for the origins of the screwdriver by consulting the *Oxford English Dictionary*. According to the citation, the first appearance in print of *screwdriver* was in 1812, in a book titled *Mechanical Exercises*. My university library has an original copy. It is a self-help manual for budding artisans written by a Glaswegian, Peter Nicholson. At the back of the book, in a list of definitions, I find the quote: "Screw Driver: a tool used to turn screws into their places."[1] Simple enough. Unfortunately, the author does not include an illustration. Nor does he mention the screwdriver anywhere else in the book; he either thought that the tool was little used—or else he took it for granted.

In the introduction, Nicholson acknowledges his debt to Joseph Moxon, the author of the first systematic account in English of craftsmen's tools and methods, published more than a hundred years earlier. Moxon, a friend of the diarist Samuel Pepys, was a printer by trade. His London shop, "under the Sign of Atlas in

Warwick Lane," sold not only books, but also maps, nautical charts, globes, and mathematical instruments. In 1678, to expand his business, Moxon began publishing how-to-do-it pamphlets for carpenters, bricklayers, and joiners. The booklets appeared monthly and sold for sixpence. In 1693, he compiled the series into a book. The 238 octavo pages, including eighteen copperplate engravings, was titled *Mechanick Exercises*.

The endearing subtitle of Moxon's book is "The Doctrine of Handy-Works." "I may safely tell you," the author advises in the preface, "that these are the *Rules* that every one that will endeavour to perform them must follow; and that by the true observing them, he may, according to his stock of *Ingenuity* and *Diligence*, sooner or later, inure his hand to the *Cunning* or *Craft* of working like a *Handy-Craft*."² Moxon begins his book by discussing smithing, "which comprehends not only the *Black-Smith's Trade*, but takes in all the trades which use either *Forge* or *File*, from the *Anchor-Smith*, to the *Watch-Maker;* they all working by the same Rules, tho' not with equal exactness, and all using the same *Tools*." Moxon describes a screw-pin and a screw-plate, crude taps and dies used to make nuts and bolts to attach strap hinges to wooden doors. The bolts have square heads and are tightened with a wrench, which may be why Moxon does not mention a screwdriver, here or anywhere else in his book.

I keep looking. There are false leads. I come across a reference to an ancient Greek dedicatory epigram that describes the tools of a carpenter and includes not only a plane and a hammer but also "four screwdrivers."[3] Since the author lived in the third century B.C., this would make the screwdriver ancient after all. I consult a classical scholar at the university. He points out that the Greek word translated as "screwdrivers" really means "tools to make holes," for the "dowels" that are mentioned in the same line. So, not screwdrivers—bow drills.

A comment in an addendum to a history of wood-working tools leads me to the entry on "Navigation" in the third edition of the *Encyclopaedia Britannica*. In an illustration of a sextant and its accessories—inter-changeable lenses, a magnifying glass, a key for adjusting the central mirror—is a clearly labeled wood-handled screwdriver.[4] The third edition was published in 1797, which is fifteen years earlier than Nicholson's *Mechanical Exercises*. I find an even older reference in the tenth edition of the *Merriam-Webster's Collegiate Dictionary*. The citation quotes a York County, Virginia, will: "1 doz. draw rings, screw driver, and gimlet."[5] No illustration this time, but the date is April 28, 1779, thirty-three years before Nicholson. So, the *OED* is not infallible.

Raphael A. Salaman's *Dictionary of Tools* of 1975 is probably the most complete modern work of its kind. The British compilation includes several specialized screwdrivers: a slender electrician's screwdriver; a tiny jeweler's screwdriver; a stubby gunmaker's screwdriver; and a short, heavy undertaker's screwdriver for fastening coffin lids. Salaman dates the origin of the screwdriver slightly earlier than the *Encyclopaedia Britannica:* "Wood screws were not extensively used by carpenters until the mid eighteenth century, and consequently the Screwdriver does not appear to have been commonly employed until after that time."[6] If screws were in use by 1750, I should be able to find a reference to screwdrivers earlier than 1779.

Something else catches my eye. Salaman writes that "although nowadays the generally accepted name is Screwdriver, it appears from the trade catalogues and other literature that, at least in the Midlands and the North of England, the usual name was Turnscrew."[7] This is news to me. I can't find an entry for *turnscrew* in any of my dictionaries. Yet Salaman is unequivocal. This raises an interesting question. *Turnscrew,* if such a word really exists, would be a literal translation of *tournevis,* French for "screwdriver." Maybe the screwdriver was invented in France?

In an encyclopedia of arts and crafts published in Paris in 1772, I find an entry by A. J. Roubo, a master cabinetmaker, who describes in detail how screws— "sold ready made"—are countersunk in brass plates and moldings inlaid into furniture. "The head of the screw is turned by means of a screwdriver," he writes.[8] The *tournevis* illustrated in an accompanying engraving is not the familiar hand tool but a flat-tipped bit for a carpenter's brace. The brace actually makes an excellent screwdriver, since the crank of the handle greatly increases the torque and the continuous turning motion prevents the screw from "freezing" in the wood. So, the first screwdriver may have been simply a modified drill bit. Maybe my essay should be about the brace *and* the screwdriver?

An obvious place to look for French technology is Diderot and d'Alembert's great *Encyclopédie*. My university's library again comes through with a complete set, all seventeen volumes, as well as eleven volumes of plates and the seven supplementary volumes. The librarian unlocks the glass case in the Rare Book Room and I heft the heavy folio over to a reading table. I open the old book carefully. The paper feels coarse. The authors of the *Encyclopédie* provide no fewer than three entries under *Tourne-vis*. First a general description, ending with the observation that "the screwdriver is a very useful tool."[9] Then a brief mention of the arquebusier's screwdriver, used by soldiers to adjust matchlock guns. Last, a long paragraph on the cabinetmaker's screwdriver. The description of the latter is characteristically thorough: the steel of the blade must be tempered for strength; the tip is to be sharp so that it won't slip out of

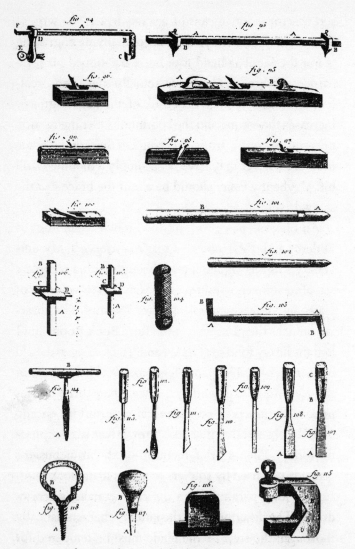

Tourne-vis from Diderot and d'Alembert's *Encyclopédie*, 1765.

the slot in the head of the screw; a metal ferrule, or band, is required to reinforce the base of the wooden handle; and the handle itself must be slightly flattened so that it can be firmly held while screwing. The text closes with a reference to an illustration. Excitedly I find the correct volume and turn to a chapter devoted to tools used by cabinetmakers and workers in marquetry. There it is at the bottom of the page. An engraving of a short-bladed tool with a flat, oval wooden handle, just as described in the text. The folio was published in 1765, fourteen years before the Virginia will, which makes it the oldest evidence of a screwdriver that I have come across so far. I'm not sure what I expected, but I'm disappointed that the tool resembles an ordinary modern screwdriver. Can this really be the first screwdriver?

Next to the engraving of the screwdriver in the *Encyclopédie* is an illustration of a curious tool that consists of a screw attached to a ring. It is identified as a *tire-fond*, which the authors explain is used by inlay workers and cabinetmakers to pull pieces of wood into place. On the same page is a description of a *tire-bouchon* (literally, cork-puller): "a kind of screw of iron or steel that is attached to a ring." For centuries, wine bottles were sealed with wooden bungs. In the mid-1600s, it was discovered that the elastic outer bark of the cork oak, which grows predominantly in Spain and Portugal, made a more effective stopper. However, the new, tight-fitting "corks" were difficult to draw. Someone—perhaps a thirsty cabinetmaker—found that the *tire-fond* made a convenient corkscrew. My old *Dictionnaire Général de la Langue Française* records the first use of *tire-bouchon* in 1718, two years before *corkscrew* appeared in English. For a moment I toy with nominating the corkscrew as the best tool of the millennium—certainly the most agreeable—but decide to continue my search.

My *Dictionnaire* states that the word *tournevis* was officially accepted by the Académie Française in 1740 and first appeared in print as early as 1723, which anticipates the first English-language reference by more than fifty years.[10] That makes sense. I had read that Moxon copied many of his illustrations from earlier French publications. It is beginning to look as if the screwdriver might be a French invention.

The first screwdrivers were probably handmade by local blacksmiths. Yet, as the engraving in the *Encyclopédie* made clear, there was nothing primitive about these early tools. Not that the screwdriver is complicated—there are many traditional tools from which it could easily have been derived. For example, the *Encyclopédie* mentions that the *tournevis* was often confused with the *tourne à gauche*, a wood-handled steel spike that was used as a key to turn other tools. Awls, files, and chisels could also have provided models for the screwdriver. Or the earliest screwdriver may simply have been a modification of a broken or disused implement. The Colonial Williamsburg Foundation owns two such screwdrivers: one is made from the broken blade of a colchimarde, or small sword; the other is adapted from an old file, with a stubby wooden handle mounted transversely, like an auger handle.[11] According to Henry C. Mercer, who in 1929 wrote the first history of American tools, auger-handled screwdrivers were commonly used in the eighteenth century to release the heavy iron screw bolts that connected rails to bedposts.

I often consult Mercer's *Ancient Carpenters' Tools*. Together with Goodman's *History of Woodworking Tools* it is one of the basic texts on the history of hand tools. Mercer's book includes several photographs of nineteenth-century screwdrivers from his extensive collection of early American tools and artifacts. Unfortunately, he has nothing new to say about the origin of the screwdriver. He has never heard of ancient Roman screwdrivers or seen medieval pictures of screwdrivers. He, too, writes that screwdrivers were not commonly used by carpenters before the nineteenth century. Nevertheless, Mercer conjectures that screwdrivers must have been used before 1700, and he speculates that Moxon may simply have overlooked the tool. I find myself agreeing with Mercer: if there were screws, there must have been screwdrivers.

Henry Chapman Mercer is an interesting figure. He was born in 1856 in Doylestown, the seat of Bucks County, Pennsylvania. He attended Harvard, where he studied art history under Charles Eliot Norton, then went on to law school. He was admitted to the bar, but thanks to a small inheritance, he was able to spend the next decade in leisurely European travel. His chief legacy of this idle period was an appreciation for the arts, an interest in antiquity, and a case of venereal disease that would prevent him from marrying. After his return to the United States, he worked as a curator of American archaeology at the University of Pennsylvania museum. At this time he appears to be an unremarkable type: the gentlemanly amateur. Photographs show a dapper young man with curly mustaches. "A good fellow: a member of the Rittenhouse Club: a collector and traveler: a man of means," is how one acquaintance described him.[12] Then Mercer showed an independent streak. He developed an original theory of archaeology, reasoning that the past could best be understood not by examining prehistory but by working back from the present. He left the university, returned to Doylestown, and began collecting early American tools.

Mercer's interest in old crafts led him to traditional ceramics. He visited England and met a tile maker who had worked for William Morris, and on his return he established an art pottery that he called the Moravian

Pottery and Tile Works. Mercer fell under the spell of the British Arts and Crafts movement. Many craft-based enterprises in furniture, metalwork, and weaving, as well as ceramics, were founded in America at this time, a reaction to the shoddy products of mass production and industrialization. Like Morris, whose handicraft business flourished, Mercer achieved not only artistic but also financial success. So-called Mercer tiles became famous and were used in prominent buildings throughout Philadelphia and the Northeast. Isabella Stewart Gardner's palatial Boston home, Fenway Court (now the Gardner Museum), owes much of its charm to a profusion of Mercer tiles.

In 1907, enriched by a second inheritance, Mercer built a home for himself. Fonthill was traditional in conception, but it was not built of traditional materials. Encouraged by his brother William, a sculptor who had been experimenting with cement, Mercer chose reinforced concrete as his primary building material. Frank Lloyd Wright would complete Unity Temple in Oak Park out of concrete the following year, but Mercer, who designed his house himself, used the new material differently—in a free-flowing and sculptural manner that recalls the Barcelona architect Antonio Gaudí. When Mercer, who personally oversaw the construction, completed his mansion—it took him four years— he followed it with a pottery works adjacent to the house, then turned his hand to building a museum to house his vast collection of tools and artifacts.

Doylestown is not far from where I live, and I decide to visit the Mercer Museum. It stands in the center of town. The building is a seven-story pile of gray concrete surmounted by clay-tiled towers, gables, and parapets. It resembles a baronial castle transplanted from the Transylvanian Alps. The unusual interior is dominated by a tall room rising to the roof and surrounded on all sides by stairs and galleries. This central space is crammed with an astonishing array of objects: high-back chairs suspended from the ceiling; rakes, hoes, and wagon wheels fixed to the walls; a wooden sleigh that floats through the air and almost crashes into a New Bedford whaleboat. The main floor contains carriages, wagons, and a cigar-store Indian standing next to a large apple press.

The guidebook informs me that there are fifty thousand objects in the museum. I had hoped to find a case with screwdrivers, but Mercer did not organize his collection according to simple categories. Instead, he created a series of small alcoves, each resembling a workshop dedicated to a different craft or occupation. I peer through the small-paned shop windows; the mullions, like everything else, are concrete. In the wheelwright's workshop I recognize a huge adze for routing axle holes; elsewhere, I glimpse a massive Commander maul. The watchmaker's shop contains several interesting miniature lathes powered by the same sort of bows that the Egyptians used to turn drills. In the woodworker's shop I see an assortment of wooden carpenter's braces as well as a giant five-foot-long plane for finishing floor planks. The room contains so many tools that the effect is dizzying—a vast nineteenth-century garage sale. Eventually, in the gunsmith's shop, I find a screwdriver. Like almost everything else, it is unlabeled.

It is December and I am the only visitor in the cavernous, cold building. Before leaving I drop into the museum library, run by the Bucks County Historical Society, to which Mercer presented the museum after its completion. Several people are working at long tables. It is the only part of the building that is heated; I will at least get warm and perhaps come across something useful. The card index has only two entries for screwdrivers, both books that I have read. There are several copies of Mercer's own book, as well as reprints of Moxon and other standard texts familiar to me.

Browsing through the stacks, I come across a book on nineteenth-century English tool manufacturers in Sheffield. This privately published book—its typed pages bound in a heavy leather cover—is relatively recent, but it is unlikely I would have found it elsewhere; it is one of only 750 copies printed.[13] Inside are reproductions of pages from English tool manufacturers' cat-

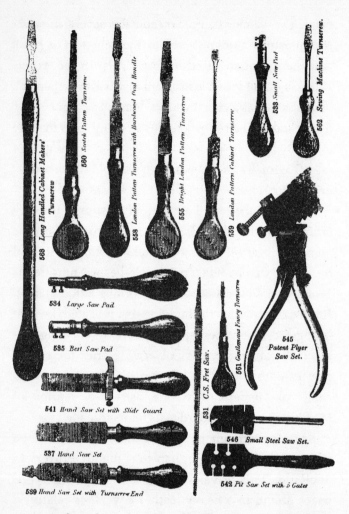

A page from the tool catalog of William Marples & Sons,
Sheffield, 1870.

alogs. Sheffield, then the center of the British steel industry, produced probably the finest tools in the world.
According to the author, Kenneth Roberts, the oldest
surviving example of a Sheffield price list is dated 1828.
There, among spokeshaves and squares, I find not one
but a whole family of screwdrivers: three inches to fourteen inches long, in black or bright finishes, and in two
patterns, Scotch (flat, tapered blades) and London (more
elaborate, waisted blades). The prices vary from four
shillings and sixpence to twenty-two shillings a dozen;
evidently the list was for job-lot buyers. Later catalogs
include illustrations of screwdrivers with flat, oval handles, just like the engraving in the *Encyclopédie*. What
surprises me, however, is the terminology: sewing
machine *turnscrew,* cabinet *turnscrew,* and a small pocket
model, the Gent's Fancy *Turnscrew*. There is even a *turnscrew* bit, for driving screws with a carpenter's brace.
There is no doubt about it. Salaman was right. Despite
its absence from my dictionaries, *turnscrew* is a real word,
perhaps an older word than *screwdriver*.

The Sheffield catalogs in Roberts's book demonstrate
that by the early 1800s, the demand for screwdrivers
was large enough to warrant factory production. The
other evidence I had found suggests that the screwdriver
appeared sometime in the previous century, perhaps in
France. *Turnscrew* is a literal translation of the French
word, and the paper trail runs out in 1723 with the

tournevis entry in my *Dictionnaire Général*. I now have enough material to write a short essay for the *New York Times,* but I have scarcely solved the puzzle of the screwdriver.[14]

CHAPTER THREE

Lock, Stock, and Barrel

THERE ARE TOOLS, such as the handsaw, that develop slowly and are refined over centuries. Others, such as the carpenter's brace, are adaptations of a new scientific principle. Then there are those inventions that appear seemingly out of the blue. The button, for example, a useful device that secures clothing against cold drafts, was unknown for most of mankind's history. The ancient Egyptians, Greeks, and Romans wore loose tunics, cloaks, and togas. Buttons were likewise absent in traditional dress throughout the Middle East, Africa, and South Asia. True, the climate in these places is mild, but northern dress was likewise buttonless. Eskimos and Vikings slipped their clothes over their heads and cinched them with belts and straps; Celts wrapped themselves in kilts; the Japanese used sashes to fasten their robes. The Romans did use buttons to ornament clothing, but the buttonhole eluded them. The ancient Chinese invented the toggle and loop, but never went on to the button and buttonhole, which are both simpler to make and more convenient to use. Then, suddenly, in the thirteenth century in northern Europe, the button appeared.[1] Or, more precisely, the button and the buttonhole. The invention of this combination—so simple, yet so cunning—is a mystery. There was no scientific or technical breakthrough—buttons can easily be made from wood, horn, or bone; the buttonhole is merely a slit in the fabric. Yet the leap of imagination that this deceptively simple device required is impressive. Try to describe in words the odd flick-and-twist motion as you button and unbutton and you realize just how complicated it is. The other mystery of the button is the manner of its discovery. It is difficult to imagine the button evolving—it either exists or it doesn't. We don't know who invented the button and the buttonhole, but he—more likely she—was a genius.

Maybe the screwdriver, like the button, is a medieval invention. I examine a book of engravings and woodcuts by the sixteenth-century artist Albrecht Dürer. Dürer occasionally portrays tools. A woodcut of the Holy Family in Egypt has Joseph using an adze to hollow out a heavy plank. In a Crucifixion scene, a man turns a large auger to drill preparatory holes for the spikes while his mate wields a heavy hammer. The fullest depiction of tools is in the famous engraving *Melancolia I*. A winged female figure is surrounded by an assortment of wood-working tools: a pair of metal dividers, an open handsaw, iron pincers, a rule, a template, a claw hammer, and four wrought-iron nails. But no screwdriver. *Melancolia I* includes several magical and allegorical objects such as an alchemist's crucible, a millstone, and an hourglass, and art historians assume that the tools in *Melancolia I* were likewise chosen for their symbolic meanings. The hammer and four nails, for example, probably refer to the Crucifixion. Maybe the screwdriver simply lacked metaphorical weight.

The most famous technological treatise of the sixteenth century was Agostino Ramelli's *Le diverse et artificiose machine* (Various and ingenious machines), published in Paris in 1588. Ramelli was an Italian mili-tary engineer who had apprenticed with the Marquis of Marigano and moved to France to serve with the Catholic League in their war against the Huguenots. He had a colorful career. During the siege of La Rochelle he was wounded and captured, but escaped—or was exchanged—and a few months later successfully mined under a bastion and breached the fortification. His commander at La Rochelle was Henri d'Anjou, who became Henri III of France, and it was to the king that Ramelli dedicated his book. Capitano Ramelli, as he styled himself, was following in the footsteps of his celebrated countryman Leonardo da Vinci, and he was no less renowned; he is described by a French contemporary as "a true Daedalus as architect and the Archimedes of our age."[2] The frontispiece of Ramelli's book shows a vigorous, bearded man holding a pair of dividers over a model of a fortification, his other, well-manicured hand resting on a steel cuirassier helmet. The author's portrait is flanked by allegorical figures symbolizing his two vocations: war and mathematics.

Ramelli's beautifully illustrated compilation of machines and technological devices was the most influential book of its kind. (Leonardo's notebooks, while celebrated today, were not published until several centuries after the author's death.) As is to be expected, the Capitano includes a number of siege engines, cunning pontoon bridges that unfold like accordions, scaling machines, and monstrous catapults. He also presents devices for clandestine break-ins: wrenches for tearing loose door bolts, giant clamps for forcing apart iron gratings and portcullises, and jacks for lifting doors off their hinges, "with great ease and little noise." The latter claim, at least, is doubtful, since there is no provision for keeping the massive door, once free of the hinge, from crashing to the ground.

The majority of the two hundred machines in his book are peaceful devices. Ramelli was fascinated by the problem of raising water and included a variety of waterwheels, pumps, and bucket conveyor belts. There are also domestic gadgets such as automatic fountains and hand-cranked machines for milling flour. The latter is important since it is the first known example of the use of rollers, rather than millstones. Ramelli's version of a revolving bookstand is particularly fascinating. Revolving bookstands were not unknown in Ramelli's day and were used by scholars consulting several heavy tomes in turn. While a conventional bookstand turned horizontally and held four books, Ramelli's six-foot-diameter bookwheel turned vertically, like a modern Ferris wheel, and could support no fewer than eight books. "This is a beautiful and ingenious machine, very useful and convenient for anyone who takes pleasure in study, especially those who are indisposed and tormented by gout," he points out with no false modesty.[3] The bookwheel was a mechanical tour de force. To ensure that the open books remained at a constant angle while the wheel turned, he incorporated a complicated epicyclic gearing arrangement, a device that had previously been used only in astronomical clocks. Of course, gravity would have done the job equally well (as it does in a Ferris wheel), but the gearing system allowed Ramelli to demonstrate his considerable skill as a mathematician.[4]

This splendid folly distracts me—I'm supposed to be looking for screwdrivers. As far as I can see, the heavy wooden bookwheel is held together with pegs. However, elsewhere in Ramelli's book, I do find screws. The iron legs of the hand-cranked flour mill are attached to a wooden base with slotted screws, one of which is

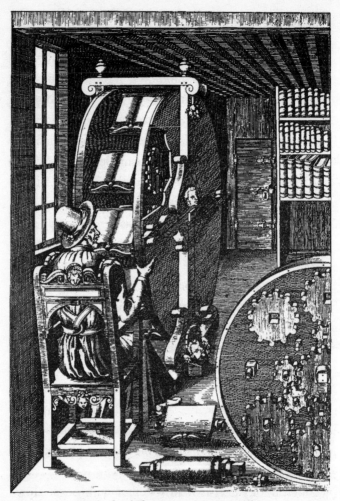

Bookwheel, from Agostino Ramelli's
Le diverse et artificiose machine, 1588.

shown partially unscrewed to reveal the threads. This is proof that screws—and presumably screwdrivers— were used more than a hundred years earlier than any of my previous sources had suggested.

Another celebrated medieval technical book is *De Re Metallica*. This treatise on mining and metallurgy was written by Georg Bauer, a Saxon scholar whose Latin-ized pen name was Georgius Agricola. Agricola, Germany's first mineralogist, laid the foundation for the systematic and scientific study of geology and mining. *De Re Metallica,* which appeared in 1556, shortly after his death, is heavily illustrated with woodcuts of mining and smelting machinery: pumps, mining hoists, and furnaces. Since many of the machines are made of wood, Agricola portrays a number of woodworking tools: axes and adzes for preparing heavy timber shoring; hammers and nails; mallets and chisels; and a long-handled auger for hollowing wooden logs into pipes.

He describes how to make the large bellows to be used for smelting iron. The woodcut illustrates the various components: the iron nozzle, the wooden boards, and the leather bellows. Ox hide is superior to horse-hide, according to the author, who goes on to advise that "some people do not fix the hide to the bellows-boards and bows by iron nails, but by iron screws, screwed at the same time through strips laid over the hide."[5] I read the passage twice. Yes, he definitely says

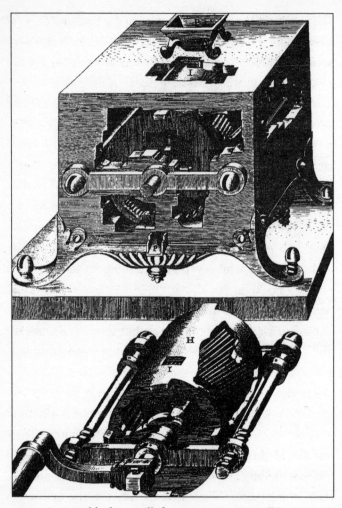

Portable flour mill, from Agostino Ramelli's
Le diverse et artificiose machine, 1588.

iron screws, and there, nestled in the bottom left-hand corner of the engraving, is a neat drawing of a screw. The tapered, threaded body is topped by a flat, slotted head. Although the means of driving the screw are not shown, Agricola provides clear evidence of the use of screws as early as the middle of the sixteenth century.

A technical work that predates both Agricola and Ramelli is the so-called *Medieval Housebook*. This handwritten manuscript, whose author and exact provenance are unknown, is thought to come from southern Germany. It has been described as a household manual for a knight's castle, a common genre at the time.[6] In its present state the book consists of sixty-three parchment leaves, beautifully illustrated and covering a variety of subjects: jousting, hunting, warfare, courtship. Astrological horoscopes describe traits of people born under the sign of different planets: the regal Sun, amorous Venus, warlike Mars. Industrious Mercury is accompanied by a variety of craftsmen: an organ builder; a goldsmith, wearing eyeglasses and hammering out a beaker; and a clockmaker. I examine the drawing through a magnifying glass, helpfully provided by the Frick Collection in New York City, where a traveling exhibition of selected pages from the *Housebook* is on display. I'm hoping to find a screwdriver on the clockmaker's workbench, but no luck. The section on smelting includes a water-powered device for working bellows, but there is no indication that screws were used. Further on, several pages are devoted to the technology of war. I pore over each drawing in turn, under the watchful eye of an increasingly suspicious museum guard.

Among the intricate drawings of cannons, battle wagons, and scaling ladders, I find a collection of miscellaneous hardware: an auger, assorted manacles, and mysteriously shaped crowbars that the caption describes as tools for forcing apart iron gratings—ancestors of Ramelli's portcullis twisters. Although the *Housebook* drawing shows a wrench, there is no screwdriver. But there is something almost as good. Two of the devices— a leg iron and a pair of manacles—are fastened with slotted screws.

The exact date of the *Housebook* is unknown. Most scholars believe that it was written between 1475 and 1490, almost a century earlier than the books of Agricola and Ramelli, and more than three hundred years before the *Encyclopédie*. Since the author of the *Housebook* included a separate drawing of a screw, one might guess that screws were a novelty. Interestingly, the screws in the *Housebook* are used to join metal, not wood. Such screws must mate with threaded holes, so these fifteenth-century screws were made with a relatively high degree of precision.

I have not found a screwdriver, but I have found a very old screw. Surely slotted screws were used for something less specialized than attaching leg irons and manacles? I go back to Dürer. Although his religious and allegorical engravings rarely include mechanical devices, an exception is his last etching, made in 1518. The subject is a cannon. It is being towed through a pastoral countryside, the roofs of a peaceful village visible in the valley below. The contrast between the artillery piece and the idyllic landscape is dramatic. This is also a comment on the mechanization of war, for the scene includes a glum-looking group of Oriental warriors holding swords and pikes. Dürer renders the cannon, its wooden carriage, and the two-wheeled limber in great detail. However, the iron parts of the cannon, including a complicated elevating mechanism, are not attached to the wooden frame with screws but with heavy spikes.

Dürer's etching gives me an idea. Weapons have often been the source of technological invention. Radar and the jet engine, which both originated during the Second World War, are two modern examples. The most dramatic military innovation of the Renaissance was the gun. The first guns were bombards, short heavy mortars firing stone balls. Bombards were fixed to wooden platforms and were dragged from place to place only with great difficulty. Before the end of the fifteenth century, however, bell foundries cast bronze barrels, about eight feet long, that were light enough to be mounted on a wheeled carriage and were fully mobile.

One of these innovative weapons is the subject of Dürer's etching.

Before casting full-size cannons, foundries experimented with small portable weapons. The oldest surviving example of such a "hand-cannon" is a one-foot-long bronze gun barrel, made in Sweden in the mid-1300s.[7] The barrel is attached to a straight wooden stock that the gunner either pressed against his body with his elbow or rested atop his shoulder like a modern antitank gun. Italians called the new weapon *arcobugio* (literally, a hollow crossbow). The Spaniards, who were leaders in gun-making, called it *arcabuz*, whence the French and English arquebus.

Firing an arquebus was tricky. After loading the gun by the muzzle, the gunner had to balance the heavy weapon with one hand while holding a smoldering match to the touchhole or firing pan with the other. Even when a forked rest or tripod was used, it was difficult to aim properly. In addition, bringing one's hand close to the priming powder was dangerous since there was always the risk of a premature explosion. Groups of arquebusiers waving burning matches while pouring gunpowder on their priming pans were likely to cause as much damage to themselves as to the enemy.

A solution to the firing problem was developed in the early 1400s. A curved metal arm holding the match was attached to the stock. In the earliest versions, the gunner manually pivoted the arm, gradually moving the match to the touchhole. Eventually, the movement was accomplished by a spring-operated mechanism, the so-called matchlock. The arm holding the match was cocked back, and when a button was depressed, a spring brought it down to the pan. In a further refinement, pressure on a lever-shaped trigger—a feature adapted from the crossbow—slowly lowered the match into the pan. Now the gunner had both hands free to steady and aim the gun. The modern firearm had arrived—lock, stock, and barrel.

The arquebus quickly became popular. In 1471, the army of the duke of Burgundy counted 1,250 armored knights, 1,250 pikemen, 5,000 archers, and 1,250 arque-busiers.[8] By 1527, in a French expeditionary force of eight hundred soldiers, more than half were arque-busiers.[9] Gunners were common soldiers. Technological innovation often trickles down from the rich to the poor; firearms evolved in the opposite direction. The first arquebuses were disdained by the nobility as unwieldy, and too inaccurate for hunting. Only in the late 1500s did the gun become a gentleman's weapon.

I go to the arms and armor gallery of the Metropolitan Museum of Art in New York City to see these early firearms for myself. In a glass case I find a matchlock made in Italy in the 1570s. The gun is about three and a half feet long with an odd-shaped, curved wooden stock that resembles a field-hockey stick. This type of gun, known as a petronel, was developed by the French, who called it a *poitrinal,* since the stock was shaped to rest against the *poitrine* (chest). Petronels were short-lived—as a skeptical English soldier pointed out, "fewe or none could abide their recoyling"—and they were replaced by guns with so-called Spanish stocks, which rested against the shoulder.[10]

The petronel in the Metropolitan is elaborately orna-

A musketeer firing his matchlock, 1607.

mented and was obviously intended for hunting. The steel barrel and lock are engraved, and the stock is inlaid with carved bone. As I look closely at the decorations, my eye is drawn to the lock. The slotted heads of two screws are plainly visible. The lock is screwed—definitely screwed—to the stock.

Screws were probably used instead of nails to ensure that the lock was not loosened by the vibration of successive detonations. This use must have happened early, certainly before the 1570s. Since there are no older matchlocks in the Metropolitan, I consult a well-known reference book, *Pollard's History of Firearms*. I find a detailed view of a matchlock in a drawing made in Nuremberg in 1505.[11] The moving parts are fixed with rivets, but the mechanism itself is fastened to the stock with four screws, just like the petronel. In this exploded view the screws are shown in their entirety. They have round, slotted heads and threaded cores tapering to sharp points. The oldest depiction of a matchlock in *Pollard's* is from a fifteenth-century German manuscript. The stubby weapon resembles a modern sawn-off shotgun. The short barrel sits in a wooden stock whose slightly angled butt suggests that the principle of transforming some of the shock of recoil into vertical movement was beginning to be understood. The precise drawing shows the right side of the gun. The lock is similarly attached to the stock with two slotted screws. The manuscript is dated 1475, about the same period as the *Medieval Housebook*.[12] Here, at last, is a widespread application of early screws.

During the 1500s, the matchlock was replaced by a new type of lock—the so-called wheel lock. The wheel, which was on a spring, was wound up, or "spanned." The key used to turn the wheel was called a spanner (which is what the English still call a wrench). When the trigger was pulled, the wheel turned rapidly against a piece of iron pyrites, producing a spark (the same principle as a modern cigarette lighter). The spark ignited the priming powder and the gun discharged. The piece of pyrites was held in a set of jaws that were tightened with small screws, and since it was necessary to regularly replace the worn pyrites, the gunner needed to have a screwdriver with him at all times. The solution was a

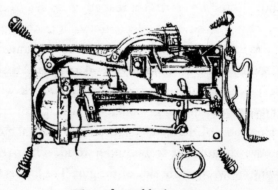

View of matchlock, 1505.

combination tool: the end of the spanner handle was flattened to serve as a screwdriver. This must be the "arquebusier's screwdriver" mentioned in Diderot's *Encyclopédie*.

The matchlocks at the Metropolitan Museum are displayed in a small room that is part of a large area devoted to arms and armor. After examining the guns I decide to take a look at the armor. This is not research—I simply have fond boyhood memories of reading Ivanhoe and seeing the Knights of the Round Table at the movies. The centerpiece of the main gallery is a group of knights mounted on armored steeds. The armor, which was tinned to prevent rusting, is shiny. There are banners and colorful pennants, which give the display a jaunty, festive air; it is easy to forget that much of this is killing dress. The day I visit, the place is full of noisy, excited schoolchildren. I stop at a display case containing a utilitarian outfit, painted entirely black—not the Black Knight, just a cheap method of preventing rust. The beak-shaped helm has only a narrow slit for the eyes. "Neat!" the boy beside me exclaims to his companion. "It's just like Darth Vader."

The display is German armor from Dresden, dated between 1580 and 1590. This is slightly later than what is generally considered to have been the golden age of armor, which lasted from about 1450 to 1550. Contrary to the movies of my boyhood, King Arthur's knights, who lived in the sixth century, would have worn chain mail, not steel armor. Protective steel plates came into use only at the end of the thirteenth century. First the knees and shins were covered, then the arms, and by about 1400, the entire body was encased. The common method of connecting the steel plates was with iron, brass, or copper rivets. When a small amount of movement was required between two plates, the rivet was set in a slot instead of a hole. Removable pieces of armor were fastened with cotter pins, turning catches, and pivot hooks; major pieces, such as the breastplate and backplate, were buckled together with leather straps.

The Dresden suit is identified as jousting armor. Jousting, or tilting, originated in martial tournaments in which groups of mounted knights fought with lance, sword, and mace. By the sixteenth century, this rude free-for-all had evolved into a highly regulated sport. Two knights, each carrying a twelve-foot-long blunted wooden lance, rode at each other on either side of a low wooden barricade called the tilt. The aim was to unseat the opponent, have him shatter his lance, or score points by hitting different parts of the body. To protect the wearer, jousting armor was heavily reinforced and weighed more than a hundred pounds (field armor was lighter, weighing between forty and sixty pounds).

The black Dresden armor was for the *scharfrennen*, a

particularly deadly German form of joust fought with sharpened lances and particularly popular with young men. Such combat required additional protection. The helm, called a *rennhut,* covered only the head and upper part of the face. The lower part of the face and the neck were protected by the *renntartsche,* a large molded plate that extended down to cover the left shoulder and was attached to the breastplate. A small shield, called a tilt targe, was fastened to the breastplate. Such "target" pieces were designed to fall off when struck; sometimes they were fitted with springs that caused them to fly dramatically into the air to the delight of the wildly applauding spectators.

Like most of the armor in the gallery, the steel plates of the Dresden suit are held together by rivets and buckled straps. Then I notice something: the *renntartsche* is screwed to the breastplate—the slotted heads, about half an inch in diameter, are plainly visible. Armorers, too, used screwdrivers! Since armor plate is relatively thin, these screws are probably mated with nuts, although I can't see them since they are hidden inside the suit. The Greenwich Armory outside London employed a dozen or more general armorers as well as a variety of specialists such as platers, millmen, helmsmiths, mail-makers, and locksmiths. It was probably the latter who fabricated the screws (medieval locks sometimes used threaded turning mechanisms).

We can be fairly sure how these screws and nuts were fabricated. In *Mechanick Exercises*, Moxon includes a section titled "The Making of Screws and Nuts," a process that could not have changed much since the Middle Ages. He describes how, after the head and shank are hammered out of a forged blank, the "screw-pin," that is, the thread, is cut with a die called a screw plate. The screw plate, made of tempered steel, has several threaded holes of different diameters. The blank is placed in a vise, and the screw plate is forced down hard and turned to cut the threads. (The corresponding nut is threaded with a tap, a tapered screw fitted with a handle.) *"Screw the Nut in the Vise directly flat, that the hole may stand upright, and put the Screw-tap upright in the hole;* then if your *Screw-tap* have a *handle,* turn it by the *handle* hard round in the *Hole,* so will the *Screw-tap* work it self into the *Hole,* and make *Grooves* in it to fit the *Threds* [*sic*] of the *Screw-pin.*"[13] Moxon's complicated instructions underline the combination of delicacy and brute strength that was needed to make a screw in this fashion.

Looking more closely at the Dresden armor, I see that the helm is attached to the backplate by large wing nuts. Since the highest points in a joust were accorded to a hit to the helm, special precautions had to be taken to protect the head. Field helms were close-fitting and worn over a coif of chain mail; the heavy jousting helm, on the other hand, did not touch the head. It was supported on the shoulders like a modern deep-sea diver's helmet and attached to the breastplate and back-plate with leather straps to keep from getting knocked off. "In suits for the joust or tourney these adjustable fastenings could not always be depended upon," observes Charles Ffoulkes in a 1912 book on armor, "and the great helm . . . [was] often screwed on to the suit."[14] Wing nuts, such as the ones on the Dresden armor, were a later refinement that allowed the exact angle of the helm to be closely adjusted. This was important. The so-called frog-mouth helm had a nar-row, beaklike viewing slit, designed so that the knight could see out as he leaned forward in the saddle, riding toward his adversary. At the last minute, just before the moment of impact, he would straightened up and the

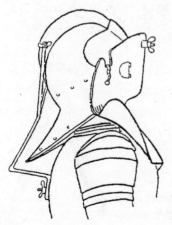

Bracket for jousting helm and protective *renntartsche*, Dresden, sixteenth century.

lower part of the helm would protect his eyes from stray splinters. It required nerve: galloping down the list, aiming the heavy lance at one's opponent who was barely visible through the helm's shaking, narrow slot, then sudden darkness followed by the jarring crash of wood against steel.

It is unclear exactly when screws were substituted for straps. Ffoulkes refers to a French military manual, written in 1446, that provides a detailed description of jousting armor. The text refers to most attachments as *cloué* (literally "nailed," as rivets were called arming nails), but in one place describes a piece as being *rivez en dedens* (fixed from the inside), which sounds like a screw and nut. I came across references to helms being screwed to breastplates as early as 1480.[15] The oldest screw in the Metropolitan Museum is part of a steel breastplate that is identified as German or Austrian and

Multipurpose armorer's tool,
sixteenth century.

dated 1480–90. If screws were used in the 1480s, that would make them the same age as the screws in the matchlock in *Pollard's History of Firearms* and the metal screws in the *Housebook*. Ffoulkes describes the heads of the screws as square or polygonal. However, all the screws I saw at the Metropolitan were slotted.

I look through Ffoulkes's chapter on "Tools, Appliances, Etc." According to the author, few armorer's tools have survived. He describes a display in the British Museum: "In the same case is a pair of armourer's pincers, which resemble the *multum in parvo* tools of today, for they include hammer, wire-cutter, nail-drawer, and turnscrew."[16] He refers to a photograph. Excitedly, I turn to plate V.[17] I had missed it earlier. Upon closer examination I can make out what looks like a pick at the end of one handle, and at the end of the other—a flat screwdriver blade. The caption beneath the photograph gives the date as the sixteenth century.

Another combination tool. I am disappointed that the oldest screwdriver resembles the kind of gimcrack household gadget that is sold by Hammacher Schlemmer. Although Ffoulkes calls this a turnscrew, like the screwdriver blade that was part of the arquebusier's spanner, it probably didn't have a special name. With so few screws, all that was needed was a part-time tool.

CHAPTER FOUR

The Biggest Little Invention

IN SEARCHING FOR the first screwdriver I have become interested in screws. When Agricola compared the screw to the nail as a way of constructing bellows, he observed that "there is no doubt that it [the screw] surpasses it in excellence."[1] In fact, the wrought-iron nail is a remarkable fastener. It bears little resemblance to the modern steel nail. The modern nail is round and pointed and forces itself between the wood fibers. Such nails are reasonably effective when driven into softwood (spruce, pine, fir), but will usually split hardwood (maple, birch, oak). Moreover, even in softwood the holding power of a round nail is weak, since it is kept in place only by the pressure of the fibers along two sides. The wrought-iron nail, on the other hand, is square or rectangular in cross-section with a hand-filed chisel point. The chisel point, driven across the grain, cuts through the wood fibers rather than forcing its way between them, just like a modern railroad spike. Such nails can be driven into the hardest wood without splitting it, and they are almost impossible to remove, as I discovered when I nailed a replica wrought-iron ship's nail into a board as an experiment.*

Wrought-iron nails have limitations, however. If they are driven into a thin piece of wood, such as a door, their holding power is greatly reduced and their protruding ends must be clenched—bent over—to keep them fast. Wrought-iron nails are most effective—and easier to fabricate—when they are relatively large (at least an inch or two long). That is why the earliest screws replaced nails in small-scale applications such as fixing leather to a bellows board, or attaching a matchlock to a gunstock. Even a short screw has great holding power. Unlike a nail or a spike, a screw is not held by friction but by a mechanical bond: the interpenetration of the sharp spiral thread and the wood fibers. This bond is so strong that a well-set screw can be removed only by destroying the surrounding wood.

The problem with screws in the sixteenth century was that, compared to nails, they were expensive. A blacksmith could turn out nails relatively quickly. Taking a red-hot rod of forged iron, he squared, drew, and

*At the beginning of the nineteenth century, handmade nails were replaced by cut nails, stamped out of sheets of wrought iron (later steel), with a similar rectangular cross-section. Cut nails are sharpened by hand with a file.

tapered the rod to a point, pushed the reheated nail through a heading tool, then with a heavy hammer formed the head. The whole procedure, which had been invented by the Romans and was still used in the 1800s (Thomas Jefferson's slaves produced nails this way at Monticello), took less than a minute, especially for an experienced "nailsmith." Making a screw was more complicated. A blank was forged, pointed, and headed, much like a nail, but round instead of square. Then a slot was cut into the head with a hacksaw. Finally, the thread was laboriously filed by hand.

Gunsmiths manufactured their own screws, just as armorers made their own bolts and wing nuts. What about clockmakers? Turret clocks appeared in Europe as early as the fourteenth century. The oldest clock of which we have detailed knowledge was built by an Italian, Giovanni De 'Dondi. It is an astronomical clock of extraordinary complexity. The seven faces show the position of the ancient planets: the Sun, Moon, Mercury, Venus, Mars, Jupiter, and Saturn; in addition, one rotating dial indicates religious feast days, and another displays the number of daylight hours in the day. De 'Dondi fashioned the bronze, brass, and copper parts by hand. It took him sixteen years to build the clock, which he finished in 1362. Although the original was destroyed by fire in the sixteenth century, the inventor left detailed instructions, and two working replicas were built in London in 1962. One of these now belongs to the National Museum of American History, and I catch up with it in Montreal, where it is part of a temporary exhibit. The exquisite seven-sided machine stands about four feet tall; the gearwheels are driven by suspended weights. I examine the mechanism. As far as I can see, all the connections are pegged mortises and tenons, a detail adapted from carpentry. The projecting tenons have slot-holes into which a wedge is driven. These wedges vary in size from tiny needlelike pins to one inch long. There must be several hundred such attachments, but I can't see a single screw.

According to *Britten's Old Clocks and Watches and Their Makers*, the standard work of horological history originally published in 1899, "screws were entirely unknown in clocks before 1550."[2] Their introduction was a result of the demand for smaller and lighter domestic clocks, especially watches. According to *Britten's*, "Even the earliest watches generally possess at least one screw. These screws have dome-shaped heads and the slots are V-shaped. The thread is coarse and irregular."[3]

By the mid-sixteenth century, applications for screws had grown to include miniature screws and bolts in watches, larger screws in guns, and heavy bolts in armor. Yet it was another two hundred years before demand grew enough that a screw industry developed.

The *Encyclopédie* mentions that the region of Forez, near Lyon, specialized in screws, which were available in a variety of lengths—one-half inch to four or five inches. These screws were still so expensive that they were sold individually. According to the *Encyclopédie*, heads were either slotted or square.

In England, screw-making was concentrated in the Midlands. It was organized as a cottage industry. Forged-steel blanks with formed heads were made in large quantities by local blacksmiths and delivered to the so-called girder, who, with his family and an assistant or two, worked at home. The first step was to cut the slot, or "nick," into the head with a hacksaw. That was the easy part. Next the thread, or "worm," had to be filed by hand. Some girders used a spindle—a crude lathe—turning a crank with one hand and guiding a heavy cutter with the other, back and forth, back and forth. Whichever method was used, the work was slow and laborious, and since the worm was cut by eye, the result was a screw with imperfect, shallow threads. According to one contemporary observer, who had seen screw-girders at work, "The expensive and tedious character of these processes rendered it impossible for the screws to compete with nails, and consequently the sale was very small. The quality was also exceedingly bad, it being impossible to produce a well-cut thread by such means."[4]

Both Moxon and the *Encyclopédie* mention that screws are used by locksmiths to fasten locks to doors. I also come across references to eighteenth-century carpenters using screws to attach hinges, particularly the novel garnet hinge. A garnet hinge resembles a ⊢—, the vertical part being fastened to the doorjamb and the horizontal to the door. Garnet hinges, used with light cupboard doors and shutters, were screwed rather than nailed to the frame. Heavy doors, on the other hand, were hung on traditional strap hinges that extended the full width of the door and were nailed and clenched.

Strap and garnet hinges are still used today, but by far the most popular modern door hinge is the butt hinge, which is not mounted on the surface but mortised into the thick end—the butt—of the door. Butt hinges are aesthetically pleasing, being almost entirely hidden when the door is closed. They were used in France as early as the sixteenth century (butt hinges are illustrated by Ramelli), but were luxury objects, crafted by hand of brass or steel. In 1775, two Englishmen patented a design for mass-producing cast-iron butt hinges.[5] Cast-iron butt hinges, cheaper than strap hinges, had one drawback: they could not be nailed. Nails worked themselves loose as the door was repeatedly opened and closed, and since the nails were in the butt of the door, they could not be clenched. Butt hinges had to be screwed.

By coincidence, at the very moment that butt hinges were being popularized, a technique for manufacturing good-quality, inexpensive screws was being perfected. Years earlier, Job and William Wyatt, two brothers from Staffordshire in the English Midlands, had set out to improve screw-making. In 1760, they patented a "method of cutting screws of iron commonly called wood-screws in a better manner than had been heretofore practiced."[6] Their method involved three separate operations. First, while the forged blank of wrought iron was held in a rotating spindle, the countersunk head was shaped with a file. Next, with the spindle stopped, a revolving saw-blade cut a slot into the head. Finally, the blank was placed in a second spindle and the thread was cut. This was the most original part of the process. Instead of being guided by hand, the cutter was connected to a pin that tracked a lead screw. In other words, the operation was automatic. Now, instead of taking several minutes, a girder could turn out a screw—a much better screw—in six or seven *seconds*.

It took the Wyatt brothers sixteen years to raise the capital required to convert a disused water corn-mill north of Birmingham into the world's first screw factory. Then, for unexplained reasons, their enterprise failed. Maybe the brothers were poor businessmen, or maybe they were simply ahead of their time. A few years later, the factory's new owners, capitalizing on the new demand for screws created by the popularity of butt hinges, turned screw manufacturing into a phenomenal success. Their thirty employees produced sixteen thousand screws a day.[7]

Machine-made screws were not simply produced more quickly, they were much better screws. Better and cheaper. In 1800, British screws cost less than tuppence a dozen. Eventually, steam power replaced waterpower in the screw factories, and a series of improvements further refined the manufacturing process. Over the next fifty years, the price dropped by almost half; in the following two decades, it dropped by half again. Inexpensive screws found a ready market. They proved useful not only for fastening butt hinges but for any application where pieces of thin wood needed to be firmly attached, which included boatbuilding, furniture-making, cabinetwork, and coachwork. Demand increased and production soared. British screw factories, which had annually produced less than one hundred thousand gross in 1800, sixty years later produced almost 7 million gross.[8]

Take a close look at a modern screw. It is a remarkable little object. The thread begins at a gimlet point, sharp as a pin. This point gently tapers into the body of the screw, whose core is cylindrical. At the top, the core tapers into a smooth shank, the thread running out to nothing. The running-out is important since an abrupt termination of the thread would weaken the screw.

The first factory-made screws were not like this at all. For one thing, although handmade screws were pointed, manufactured screws had blunt ends and were not self-starting—it was always necessary first to drill a lead hole. The problem lay in the manufacturing process. Blunt screws could not simply be filed to a point—the thread itself had to come to a point, too. But lathes were incapable of cutting a tapering thread. Screw manufacturers tried angling the cutters, which produced screws that tapered along their entire length. Such screws had poor holding power, however, and carpenters refused to use them. What was needed was a machine that could cut a continuous thread in the body of the screw (a cylinder) and also in the gimlet point (a cone).

An inventive American mechanic found the solution. The first American screw factories had been established in Rhode Island in 1810, using adapted English machines. Providence became the center of the American screw industry, which by the mid-1830s was experiencing a boom in demand for its products. Beginning in 1837, a series of patents addressed the problem of manufacturing gimlet-pointed screws, but it took more than a decade of trial and error to get it right. In 1842, Cullen Whipple, a mechanic from Providence who worked for the New England Screw Company, invented a method of manufacturing screws on a machine that was entirely automatic. Seven years later he made a breakthrough and successfully patented a method of producing pointed screws. A slightly different technique was devised by Thomas J. Sloan, whose patent became the mainstay of the giant American Screw Company. Another New Englander, Charles D. Rogers, solved the problem of tapering the threaded core into the smooth shank. Such advances put American screw manufacturers firmly in the lead, and by the turn of the century, when the screw had achieved its final form, American methods of production dominated the globe.

Ever since the fifteenth century, screws had had either square or octagonal heads, or slots. The former were turned by a wrench, the latter by a screwdriver. There is no mystery as to the origin of the slot. A square head had to be accurate to fit the wrench; a slot was a shape that could be roughly filed or cut by hand. Screws with slotted heads could also be countersunk so they would not protrude beyond the surface—which was necessary to attach butt hinges. Once countersunk screws came into common use in the early 1800s, slotted heads—and flat-bladed screwdrivers—became standard. So, even as screws were entirely made by machine, the traditional slot remained. Yet slotted screws have several drawbacks. It is easy to "cam out," that is, to push the screwdriver out of the slot; the result is often damage to the material that is being fastened or injury to one's fingers—or both. The slot offers a tenuous purchase on the screw, and it is not uncommon to strip the slot when trying to tighten a new screw or loosen an old one. Finally, there are awkward situations—balancing on a stepladder, for example, or working in confined quarters—when one has to drive the screw with one hand. This is almost impossible to do with a slotted screw. The screw wobbles, the screwdriver slips, the screw falls to the ground and rolls away, the handyman curses—not for the first time—the inventor of this maddening device.

American screw manufacturers were well aware of these shortcomings. Between 1860 and 1890, there was a flurry of patents for magnetic screwdrivers, screw-holding gadgets, slots that did not extend across the face of the screw, double slots, and a variety of square, triangular, and hexagonal sockets or recesses. The latter held the most promise. Replacing the slot by a socket held the screwdriver snugly and prevented cam-out. The difficulty—once more—lay in manufacturing. Screw heads are formed by mechanically stamping a cold steel rod; punching a socket sufficiently deep to hold the screwdriver tended to either weaken the screw or deform the head.

The solution was discovered by a twenty-seven-year-old Canadian, Peter L. Robertson. Robertson was a so-called high-pitch man for a Philadelphia tool company, a traveling salesman who plied his wares on street corners and at country fairs in eastern Canada. He spent his spare time in his workshop, dabbling in mechanical inventions. He invented and promoted "Robertson's 20th Century Wrench-Brace," a combination tool that could be used as a brace, a monkey wrench, a screwdriver, a bench vise, and a rivet maker. He vainly patented an improved corkscrew, a new type of cuff links, even a better mousetrap. Then, in 1907, he received a patent for a socket-head screw.

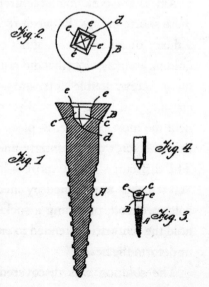

Peter L. Robertson's
1907 patent for a
socket-head screw.

Robertson later said that he got the idea for the socket head while demonstrating a spring-loaded screwdriver to a group of sidewalk gawkers in Montreal—the blade slipped out of the slot and injured his hand. The secret of his invention was the exact shape of the recess, which was square with chamfered edges, slightly tapering sides, and a pyramidal bottom. "It was early discovered that by the use of this form of punch, constructed with the exact angles indicated, cold metal would flow to the sides, and not be driven ahead of the tools, resulting beneficially in knitting the atoms into greater strength, and also assisting in the work of lateral extension, and without a waste or cutting away of any of the metal so treated, as is the case in the manufacture of the ordinary slotted head screw," he rather grandly explained.[9]

An enthusiastic promoter, Robertson found financial backers, talked a small Ontario town, Milton, into giving him a tax-free loan and other concessions, and established his own screw factory. "The big fortunes are in the small inventions," he trumpeted to prospective investors. "This is considered by many as the biggest little invention of the 20th century so far."[10] In truth, the square socket really was a big improvement. The special square-headed screwdriver fit snuggly—Robertson claimed an accuracy within one one-thousandth of an inch—and never cammed out. Craftsmen, especially furniture-makers and boatbuilders, appreciated the convenience of screws that were self-centering and could be driven with one hand. Industry liked socket-head screws, too, since they reduced product damage and speeded up production. The Fisher Body Company, which made wood bodies in Canada for Ford cars, became a large Robertson customer; so did the new Ford Model T plant in Windsor, Ontario, which soon accounted for a third of Robertson's output. Within five years of starting, Robertson built his own wire-drawing plant and powerhouse and employed seventy-five workers.

In 1913, Robertson decided to expand his business outside Canada. His father had been a Scottish immigrant, so Robertson set his sights on Britain. He established an independent English company to serve as a base for exporting to Germany and Russia. The venture was not a success. He was thwarted by a combination of undercapitalization, the First World War, the defeat of Germany, and the Russian Revolution. Moreover, it proved difficult to run businesses on two continents. After seven years, unhappy English shareholders replaced Robertson as managing director. The English company struggled along until it was liquidated in 1926. Meanwhile, Robertson turned to the United States. Negotiations with a large screw manufacturer in Buffalo broke down after it became clear that Robertson was unwilling to share control over production decisions. Henry Ford was interested, since his Canadian plants were reputedly saving as much as $2.60 per car using Robertson screws. However, Ford, too, wanted a measure of control that the stubborn Robertson was unwilling to grant. They met but no deal was struck. It was Robertson's last attempt to export his product. A lifelong bachelor, he spent the rest of his life in Milton, a big fish in a decidedly small pond.

Meanwhile, American automobile manufacturers followed Ford's lead and stuck to slotted screws. Yet the success of the new Robertson screw did not go unnoticed. In 1936 alone, there were more than twenty American patents for improved screws and screwdrivers. Several of these were granted to Henry F. Phillips, a forty-six-year-old businessman from Portland, Oregon. Like Robertson, Phillips had been a traveling salesman. He was also a promoter of new inventions, and acquired patents from a Portland inventor, John P. Thompson, for a socket screw. Thompson's socket was too deep to be practicable, but Phillips incorporated its distinctive shape—a cruciform—into an improved design of his own. Like Robertson, Phillips claimed that the socket was "particularly adapted for firm engagement with a correspondingly shaped driving tool or screwdriver, and in such a way that there will be no tendency of the driver to cam out of the recess."[11] Unlike Robertson, however, Phillips did not start his own company but planned to license his patent to screw manufacturers.

All the major screw companies turned him down. "The manufacture and marketing of these articles do not promise sufficient commercial success" was a typical response.[12] Phillips did not give up. Several years later a newly appointed president of the giant American Screw Company, which had prospered on the basis of Sloan's patent for manufacturing pointed screws, agreed to undertake the industrial development of the innovative socket screw. In his patents, Phillips emphasized that the screw was particularly suited to power-driven operations, which at the time chiefly meant automobile assembly lines. The American Screw Company convinced General Motors to test the new screw; it was used first in the 1936 Cadillac. The trial proved so effective that within two years all automobile companies save one had switched to socket screws, and by 1939 most screw manufacturers produced what were now called Phillips screws.

The Phillips screw has many of the same benefits as the Robertson screw (and the added advantage that it can be driven with a conventional screwdriver if necessary). "We estimate that our operators save between 30 and 60 percent of their time by using Phillips screws," wrote a satisfied builder of boats and gliders.[13] "Our men claim they can accomplish at least 75 percent more work than with the old-fashioned type," maintained a manufacturer of garden furniture.[14] Phillips screws—

and the familiar cross-tipped screwdrivers—were now everywhere. The First World War had stymied Robertson; the Second World War ensured that the Phillips screw became an industry standard as it was widely adopted by wartime manufacturers. By the mid-1960s, when Phillips's patents expired, there were more than 160 domestic, and 80 foreign licensees.[15]

The Phillips screw became the international socket screw; the Robertson screw is used only in Canada and by a select number of American woodworkers.* A few years ago, *Consumer Reports* tested Robertson and Phillips screwdrivers. "After driving hundreds of screws by hand and with a cordless drill fitted with a Robertson tip, we're convinced. Compared with slotted and Phillips-head screwdrivers, the Robertson worked faster, with less cam-out."[16] The explanation is simple. Although Phillips designed his screw to have "firm engagement" with the screwdriver, in fact a cruciform recess is a less perfect fit than a square socket. Paradoxically, this very quality is what attracted automobile manufacturers to the Phillips screw. The point of an automated driver turning the screw with increasing force popped out of the recess

---

*Starting in the 1950s, Robertson screws began to be used by some American furniture manufacturers, by the mobile-home industry, and eventually by a growing number of craftsmen and hobbyists. The Robertson company itself was purchased by an American conglomerate in 1968.

when the screw was fully set, preventing overscrewing. Thus, a certain degree of cam-out was incorporated into the design from the beginning. However, what worked on the assembly line has bedeviled handymen ever since. Phillips screws are notorious for slippage, cam-out, and stripped sockets (especially if the screw or the screwdriver are improperly made). Here I must confess myself to be a confirmed Robertson user. The square-headed screwdriver sits snugly in the socket: you can shake a Robertson screwdriver, and the screw on the end will not fall off; drive a Robertson screw with a power drill, and the fully set screw simply stops the drill dead; no matter how old, rusty, or painted over, a Robertson screw can always be unscrewed. The "biggest little invention of the twentieth century"? Why not.

CHAPTER FIVE

Delicate Adjustments

IN READING ABOUT the Wyatt brothers' factory in Staffordshire, I had been struck by the statement that their screw-making machines were operated by children. During the eighteenth century, children commonly worked in coal mines, workshops, and factories, but were usually given only menial tasks. Even a machine as simple as a screw girder's spindle required an experienced— not to say strong—operator. The Wyatt machines were obviously different. I had stumbled on a landmark of industrialization.[1] At a remarkably early date—the industrial revolution would not get fully under way for another hundred years—the Wyatt brothers not only pioneered the use of multipurpose machines to achieve mass production, they were the first to put into place the guiding principle of industrialization. Their factory was the earliest example of an industrial process designed specifically to shift control over the quality of what was being produced from the skilled artisan to the machine itself.

The screw girder's spindle and the Wyatt brothers' screw-making machines are both examples of simple turning-lathes. In a lathe, the blank, or workpiece, is rotated around an axis, somewhat like a potter's wheel. However, while a potter creates a shape by building up clay, the turner removes material. As the workpiece turns, a sharp cutter is applied to the surface and, depending on the desired shape, removes inequalities until every part is equidistant from the axis. The lathe is an ancient tool that appears to have been invented in Europe, since the earliest surviving pieces of lathe work are an eighth-century B.C. Etruscan bowl, and a sixth-century B.C. bowl found in Upper Bavaria.[2] Although these wooden objects were definitely turned, nothing is known of the lathes themselves. Turning technology eventually spread to the rest of the Mediterranean world, including Egypt, where the oldest depiction of a lathe, dating from the third century B.C., has been found in a bas-relief on a grave wall. The piece being turned, which appears to be a furniture leg, is held vertically. The turner's cutting tool resembles a chisel; his assistant rotates the piece by pulling a cord looped around the rotating axle, or mandrel. Since the workpiece rotates in alternate directions, the turner cuts only on every other turn.

The Egyptian bas-relief shows the turner and his assistant kneeling on the ground. It reminds me of my first visit to India, when I saw a carpenter at work squatting on the floor. Just as the world is divided into those who wrap and those who button up, or those who eat with their fingers and those who eat with utensils, it is divided into craftsmen who work kneeling, squatting, or sitting on the ground, and those who work erect—or sitting—at a bench. The ancient Egyptians belonged to the former category; the Romans, to the latter. Since the Romans invented the plane, they needed a flat surface to which the workpiece could be fastened, and the result was the first carpenter's bench.

Although Europeans in the Middle Ages often relaxed by sitting on cushions on the floor in the Oriental manner, they worked erect. This habit probably prompted the thirteenth-century European invention of the so-called pole lathe. The turner works standing up at a pole lathe. The workpiece rotates not vertically but horizontally. A cord is looped around the mandrel with one end attached to a hinged treadle, and the other fastened to a flexible pole, resembling a bowed fishing rod, that keeps the cord taut. The turner, alternately pressing and releasing the treadle with his foot, now has both hands free to guide the long-handled cutter, which he braces under his arm or over his shoulder for added stability. Like the Egyptian lathe, the pole lathe turns back and forth.

The simple pole lathe was used by wood turners for a long time—working examples survived in England until the early 1900s. For turning metal, however, a more effective machine was required. Here the screw again plays a vital role, for the ancestor of the modern lathe is in fact a machine for cutting screws. It was invented almost three hundred years before the Wyatt brothers' screw-making lathes and appears in the *Medieval Housebook*, the fifteenth-century manuscript that I had consulted in the Frick Collection. The beautiful drawing is precise. The lathe, a radical departure from the pole lathe, consists of a heavy frame mounted

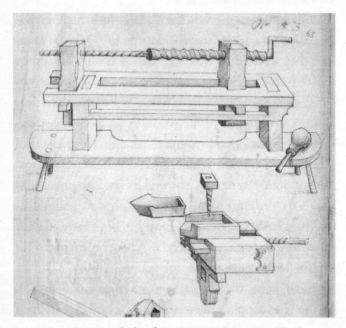

Screw-cutting lathe, from *The Medieval Housebook of Wolfegg Castle*, c. 1475–90.

on a solid workbench. The blank is held horizontally between two adjustable supports and rotated by turning a hand crank. One end of the blank is attached to a lead screw. As the blank turns, the lead screw advances through a threaded hole in one of the supports and pushes the blank through a box containing a sharp cutter that incises the thread. The operator has only to set up the blank in the jig, wedge the threaded support and the cutter-box in place, adjust the depth of the cutter, and turn the crank.

The *Housebook* lathe is made of wood, but it is a true machine tool; that is, it is a tool in which the machine—not the craftsman—controls the cutter.[3] It anticipates many features of the modern bench lathe: the two supports (today called a headstock and a tailstock); the frame (ancestor of the modern slide-rest) that allows flexibility in the location of cutter-box and stocks; a continuous drive that can be connected by a belt drive to an external power source such as a waterwheel; a rotating lead screw that advances the blank by tiny increments; a design that integrates the lathe with the workbench; and heavy construction that assures rigidity and a relatively high degree of precision.

The drawing of the lathe appears on the same manuscript page of the *Medieval Housebook* as the manacles, wrenching tools, and slotted screws. The slotted screws, which are tapered, were obviously filed by hand; the

lathe was used to turn the long wrought-iron screws
that are part of the wrenching tools. It is several weeks
since I visited the Frick, but I still have an illustrated catalog from the exhibition, and I examine the drawing of
the lathe closely, trying to understand how it works.[4]
The pointed cutter, which must have been tempered
steel, is threaded to enable the operator to adjust the
depth of the cut. It would have taken many passes to cut
a thread into a hard wrought-iron rod. After each pass,
the workpiece was retracted, the cutter was tightened to
cut a deeper groove, and the operation was repeated. A
lengthy process, but one that probably produced a reasonably accurate screw.

The drawing of the lathe includes a short-handled
tool lying on the workbench. At first I assume that it is
some sort of chisel or gouge. But as the exact function-
ing of the lathe becomes clearer, it is obvious that a
chisel plays no part in the process. The author of the
Medieval Housebook is thorough and his drawings do not
usually contain extraneous information. While beautifully composed, these are technical documents that carefully describe how the various machines work, and
exactly what tools are needed to operate them. A view of
a spinning wheel, for example, includes a couple of
empty spools. So what is the function of the mysterious
tool? One day, while I am puzzling over the drawing
again, I realize that the blunt end is exactly the same size

as the slot in the head of the cutter. Of course. It's not a chisel, it's used to adjust the cutter. It's a screwdriver.

Eureka! I've found it. The first screwdriver. No improvised gadget but a remarkably refined tool, complete with a pear-shaped wooden handle to give a good grip, and what appears to be a metal ferrule where the metal blade meets the handle. Since the *Housebook* was written during the last quarter of the fifteenth century, there is no doubt that a full-fledged screwdriver existed three hundred years *before* the tool portrayed in the *Encyclopédie*. This confirms what I had suspected: the screwdriver and the screw were invented at about the same time. My guess about fifteenth-century armorers and gunsmiths was not far off the mark either. The *Housebook* lathe is illustrated in a chapter devoted to the technology of war, so it is likely that screwdrivers appeared first in military workshops, though perhaps not in France, as I had assumed, but in Germany.*

For some reason, the potential of the *Housebook* lathe was not immediately recognized. Perhaps the unknown inventor did not publicize his lathe; as far as we know, the *Housebook* existed in only one copy, and medieval crafts-

---

*The old German word for screwdriver is *schraubendreher* (screw-turner), which originally meant the craft of turning screws, but came to refer to the tool itself.

men were often possessive about their work. Yet it appears that Leonardo da Vinci, at least, was aware of the innovative lathe, for in the early 1500s he designed a number of screw-making machines, one of which bears a striking resemblance to the earlier machine. Characteristically, Leonardo made improvements. Instead of advancing the blank through the cutter, he made the cutter move along the rotating blank, as it does in a modern lathe. Further, by using different interchangeable gears (four are shown in his sketch), he could make the cutter advance at different rates. Since the blank was turning at a constant rate, if the cutter moved more slowly, the pitch (the distance between the threads) of the resulting screw was smaller; if the cutter moved more quickly, the pitch was larger. Thus, the same machine could make screws with four different pitches. As with so many of Leonardo's inventions, it is unclear if this remarkable machine was actually built.

Leonardo da Vinci's screw-cutting machine, c. 1500.

Although Agostino Ramelli worked in France, Leonardo's actual successor as engineer to the French court was Jacques Besson, who designed several screw-cutting lathes.[5] Besson's lathes were extremely elaborate, turned not by means of a crank but by pulling on counterweighted cords. This produced the old-

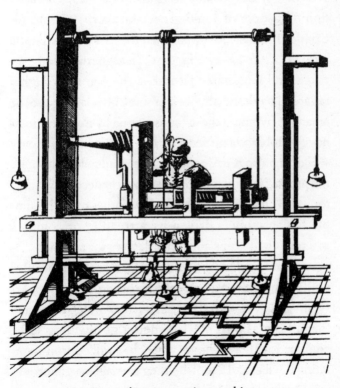

Jacques Besson's screw-cutting machine, 1579.

fashioned alternating rotation and also resulted in slippage and a loss of power. But efficiency was not uppermost in Besson's mind, for his machines were not intended for industrial workers but for hobbyists. Turning had become the gentleman's equivalent of needlepoint and remained in vogue as a pastime until the end of the eighteenth century. "It is an established fact that in present-day Europe this art is the most serious occupation of people of intelligence and merit," wrote Fr. Charles Plumier, who published the first treatise on the lathe, *L'art de tourner,* in 1701, "and, between amusements and reasonable pleasures, the one most highly regarded by those who seek in some honest exercise the means of avoiding those faults caused by excessive idleness."[6] Hobbyists turned a variety of materials, not only wood, but also horn, copper, silver, and gold. Although the products of their labors were purely decorative, they took their machines seriously. The lathes could be simple bench models driven by a treadle, or complex machines with cams and other devices for making elaborate forms, including ornamental screws. The so-called guilloching lathe was capable of tracing complex intertwining curves onto flat disks such as watch cases and medallions. Louis XVI owned a guilloching lathe equipped with a mahogany bench, a gilded iron regulating device, and a tool-holding carriage of gilt bronze inset with the royal coat of arms.[7]

Aristocrats used lathes to fill their idle hours, but for others, precision lathework was a purposeful occupation. In 1762, a London instrument-maker named Jesse Ramsden began a project that would revolutionize the lathe. Ramsden, born in Yorkshire in 1735, had originally been apprenticed to a cloth-maker. When he was twenty-three, he unexpectedly quit his trade and went to London to work for a maker of mathematical instruments. Four years later, he opened his own business. Now, to make his mark, he set out to solve a problem that plagued instrument-making: graduated scales. Linear scales, subdivided into standard measures, were a key ingredient of sextants, theodolites, and instruments used in astronomical observation. Graduated scales were traditionally made by hand and hence lacked accuracy. Ramsden designed a scale-dividing machine that was capable of engraving scales with great precision.

The machine incorporated long, fine-threaded regulating screws of microscopic accuracy. Regulating screws, the refined relatives of ordinary screws, convert rotation into minute horizontal movement by means of tracking pins or nuts. To ensure accuracy, the threads must meet stringent requirements: pitch must be constant; the cores must be exactly parallel and concentric; and the friction against the adjusting nut must be minimal but steady. In other words, these screws must be perfect.

Since screws of such precision were not available,

Ramsden set out to make them himself. It was a daunting problem: how to produce a perfect screw using a lathe with an imperfect lead screw. Patiently, he produced a succession of screws of increasingly greater accuracy. In the process, he made important improvements to the lathe. At a time when most instrument-makers still used wooden pole lathes, he built bench lathes entirely of steel. He invented a triangular slide bar, which gave more accuracy, and he was also the first to use diamond-tipped cutting tools. He finally was able to produce a screw with a claimed accuracy of one four-thousandth of an inch. In all, it took him eleven years to build his dividing machine.

Ramsden's achievement had enormous implications. Accurate regulating screws were incorporated into a variety of precision instruments and opened up new worlds to science as they facilitated the work not only of astronomers, but also of physicists, who depended on

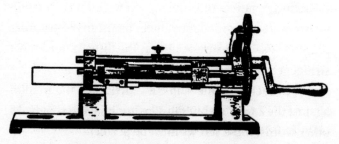

Jesse Ramsden's precision screw-cutting lathe, 1777.

accurate regulating screws in microscopes. Other new worlds were opened up, too. The navigation instrument most affected by Ramsden's work was the sextant. A sextant incorporates an arclike graduated scale that spans sixty degrees (one-sixth of a circle, whence the Latin root *sextus*), a movable radial arm, and a fixed telescope. The navigator "shooting the sun" lines up the horizon in the telescope, then adjusts a mirror attached to the radial arm until he sees a reflection of the sun. The angle between the mirror and the telescope, which is read off the graduated scale, corresponds to the angle of the sun above the horizon. With this information, and the aid of published tables, the exact latitude can be computed. Thanks to Ramsden's scale-dividing machine, it was possible to know a ship's position to within ten seconds of latitude, or about a thousand feet. Such accuracy facilitated the feats of navigation and great voyages of discovery of explorers like Captain Cook.

Ramsden was working on his screw-cutting lathes in London at the same time the Wyatt brothers were organizing their screw factory in Staffordshire. The scientific instrument-maker's precision machines and the crude factory lathes both used regulating screws, but they existed in two different realms. These realms were soon to meet, thanks to the inventive genius of Henry Maudslay. Maudslay was born in 1771 in humble circumstances and was apprenticed to a blacksmith in the Royal Arsenal at Woolwich, near London. Unusually gifted as a metalworker, Maudslay came to the attention of Joseph Bramah, a prominent manufacturer and inventor. Bramah was looking for someone to make a prototype of his latest invention, an unpickable bank lock. The design, which incorporated numerous tumblers, was so complicated that it had confounded his own experienced craftsmen. Maudslay, then only eighteen, not only successfully built the prototype, but also designed and built the tools and machines needed to commercialize its production.*

The burly young blacksmith was a mechanical prodigy. Just as some people have a natural aptitude for chess or playing the violin, Maudslay could shape metal with a dexterity and precision that amazed his contemporaries. Moreover, he was able to intuit solutions to mechanical problems. For example, while he was building a lathe for Bramah, he invented the slide rest, a perfectly straight bar that supported a movable tool holder. Although a similar device had been suggested by Leonardo, it had never been implemented. The importance of the slide rest cannot be understated. In previous

---

*The prototype lock, prominently displayed in Bramah's shopwindow, remained unpicked for more than fifty years. It was finally cracked by an American locksmith—it took him sixteen days.

lathes, the turner guided the cutter by hand. The slide rest allowed the cutting tool to move smoothly and precisely along the length of the revolving workpiece. At first the device was greeted with scorn and nicknamed Maudslay's Go-Cart, but it proved so successful that it was soon widely copied (Maudslay rarely patented his inventions).

After eight years with Bramah, and having risen to the position of foreman, Maudslay struck out on his own. While filling orders for customers—his first commission was a metal easel for an artist—he continued to tinker with precision lathes. His first breakthrough—in 1797—was a lathe for cutting long screws that incorporated a three-foot-long regulating screw. In a later ver-

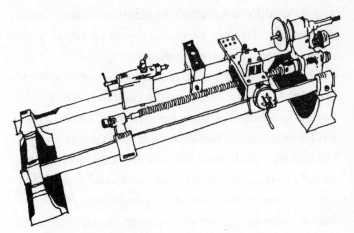

Henry Maudslay's first screw-cutting lathe, c. 1797.

sion, following once more in Leonardo's footsteps, he added interchangeable gears to produce screws of different diameter and pitch.

Thanks to a precision regulating screw displayed in his shopwindow, Maudslay met an extraordinary Frenchman, Marc Isambard Brunel. A royalist, Brunel had fled the French Revolution for America, had worked in New York as an engineer and architect, and was now settled in London. A prolific inventor—and ex–naval officer—he had a plan for manufacturing wooden ships' pulleys for the British navy. He needed someone who could build the prototype machines to demonstrate the practicality of his process. With Maudslay's help, Brunel won the contract. The factory in Portsmouth, with forty-four of Maudslay's machines, took six years to build. It was the world's first example of a fully mechanized production line. Ten men produced 160,000 pulleys a year, the navy's entire annual requirement.

Maudslay and Brunel collaborated on another venture. In 1825, Brunel received the commission to build a twelve-hundred-foot tunnel under the Thames River. Previously, tunnels had been built with temporary timber shoring, but Brunel invented an extendable, waterproof, cast-iron shield that moved ahead of the construction as the excavation progressed. Maudslay built the device. His workshop also produced a variety of specialized machines—for printing, pressing, and minting. He invented a machine for punching holes in boiler-plate (an operation previously carried out by hand) that greatly speeded up riveting. He was best known for his pioneering marine steam engines, with which he equipped at least forty vessels during his lifetime. When Isambard Kingdom Brunel, Marc's son and like-wise an engineer, built the *Great Western*, the first steamship to cross the Atlantic, it was Maudslay's firm, now run by *his* son, that built the 750-horsepower engine, the largest in the world.

The key to the success of Maudslay's workshop was the precision lathe. The *Housebook* lathe had incorpo-rated an early version of the slide rest; Leonardo had invented the moving cutter and interchangeable gears; and Plumier had described all-metal lathes. The eigh-teenth century saw many improvements to the lathe. In 1710, a Swede built a lathe for accurate cutting of iron screws; fifty years later, a Frenchman completed an industrial lathe with a traversing carriage; around 1796, a Rhode Island mechanic built an advanced lathe for screw-cutting; and, of course, Ramsden provided a strik-ing example of precision screw-cutting. Yet it was Maud-slay who synthesized all these features into a lathe capable of precision work on a large scale. In the process he produced the mother tool of the industrial age.

The heart of Maudslay's lathe was an extremely accu-rate regulating screw. He built a machine that cut threads of any pitch into soft metals such as tin and brass, then used these lead screws to make regulating screws of hard steel. "This beautiful and truly original contrivance became, in the hands of the inventor, the parent of a vast progeny of perfect screws, whose descendants, whether legitimate or not, are to be found in every workshop throughout the world, wherever first-class machinery is constructed," wrote a contemporary.[8] It is important to understand the enormous impact of precision machine tools. It was not merely a question of supplanting manual labor. Steam engines, for example, simply could not have been built by hand—cylinders and piston rods required completely new standards of perfection. Precision opened the door to a mechanical world.

On Sundays, Maudslay would tour his quiet workshops to examine the work in progress. Chalk in hand, he would jot down his comments directly on his workmen's benches. He particularly singled out examples of mechanical accuracy—or its lack. The ideal of precision was perhaps Maudslay's greatest invention. He fabricated a regulating screw used in the manufacture of scientific instruments that was five feet long and two inches in diameter and was cut with fifty threads to the inch. He built himself a micrometer with a sixteen-inch-long screw that could measure to one ten-thousandth of an inch. It was used as the ultimate dimensioning standard by Maudslay's employees, who nicknamed it the Lord

Chancellor. He provided each of his workers with a perfectly flat steel plate so that work in progress could periodically be placed on it to check if it was true. According to one of his assistants, these plates, which were filed and scraped by hand, were so smooth that "when placed over each other they would float upon the thin stratum of air between them until dislodged by time and pressure. When they adhered closely to each other, they could only be separated by sliding off each other."[9]

Maudslay also championed uniformity in screws. Surprisingly, this was a radical idea. Previously, each nut and bolt had been fabricated as a unique matching pair. "Any intermixture that occurred between them led to endless trouble and expense, as well as inefficiency and confusion," observed one of his employees, "especially when parts of complex machines had to be taken to pieces for repairs."[10] Maudslay adopted standardized taps and dies in his workshop, so that all nuts and bolts were made in a limited number of sizes. Now any nut would fit any bolt of the same size. This example inspired his pupil Joseph Whitworth, who in 1841 proposed a national standard for screw threads that eventually was adopted by all British manufacturers.*

*The Whitworth system was not international. When the United States developed its own, competing screw industry, it adopted a slightly different standard; continental Europe, which followed the metric system, likewise went its own way.

Whitworth was Maudslay's successor as Britain's great mechanical innovator. Unlike Maudslay, though, he was a manufacturer who also built specialized machine tools to order. The machine tools that came out of his factory were known throughout the world. They were versatile, dependable, and reasonably priced—and, incidentally, quite beautiful. It took a mechanical genius and a gifted craftsman like Maudslay to build the first precision lathe. Thanks to the machines that came from Whitworth's Manchester works, any well-equipped workshop could routinely achieve similar accuracy. The high standards that Maudslay had set for himself had become universal.

Maudslay died in 1831. He was interred in a cast-iron tomb of his own design. The inscription described him as "eminently distinguished as an engineer for mathematical accuracy and beauty of construction."[11] True enough, but a more moving epitaph was provided by one of his old workmen: "It was a pleasure to see him handle a tool of any kind, but he was *quite splendid* with an eighteen-inch file."[12]

CHAPTER SIX

Mechanical Bent

MAUDSLAY HAD WHAT IS often called a mechanical bent. So did the men he trained. Whitworth was the best known, but there were others: Joseph Clement, whom Charles Babbage commissioned to build his famous difference engine, the calculating machine that anticipated the modern computer; Richard Roberts, whose metal planing machine was capable of such precision that he used it to manufacture iron billiard tables; and Maudslay's personal assistant, James Nasmyth, who went on to invent the steam hammer and the pile driver. Like their master, these men generally came from modest backgrounds: Whitworth was the son of a schoolteacher; Clement's father was a weaver; Roberts's, a shoemaker. Moreover, they grew up not in cities but in small, remote villages or rural towns, without the least exposure to engineering. They often reached their calling by circuitous routes. Maudslay himself was apprenticed first to a carpenter; Roberts began as a quarryman; Clement was a slater's assistant. Despite such unpromising beginnings, all were attracted to the world of machines.

"My first essay at making a steam-engine was when I was fifteen," Nasmyth told his biographer. "I then made a real working steam-engine, $1\frac{1}{4}$ diameter cylinder, and 8-in. stroke, which not only could act, but really did some useful work; for I made it grind the oil colors which my father required for his painting."[1] Nasmyth's background was different from that of his colleagues. He was born in a large city, Edinburgh, to a prosperous family—his father was the well-known Scottish landscape painter Alexander Nasmyth. James attended the High School in Edinburgh, the School of Art, and the university. In his spare time he continued his mechanical experiments with steam engines, casting parts in his bedroom, hanging around machine shops. The municipality was debating the wisdom of adopting steam-powered carriages for public roads, and Nasmyth achieved a small measure of local renown by building a vehicle that carried eight persons. This was more than two decades after George Stephenson built the first steam road-carriage, but it was still a remarkable accomplishment for a self-taught young man not yet twenty. Finally, having determined to pursue a career in mechanical engineering, Nasmyth decided to apprentice under the famed Henry Maudslay. He traveled to London and presented himself to the great man, bringing with him a working model of a steam engine. Maudslay, who no longer took pupils, spent twenty minutes examining the beautifully made engine, then took the young man on as his personal assistant.

Maudslay recognized in Nasmyth traits shared by all these men: an innate love of mechanics, a natural aptitude for working with metals, and above all a devotion to precision. Precision was an absolute standard. Maudslay, for example, produced regulating screws of much greater accuracy than was required by industry at the time; Whitworth built himself a micrometer that was accurate to one-millionth of an inch. These men are called engineers, but this designation is inadequate. For one thing, they were working in uncharted territory in which invention as well as technical proficiency was required. They were not simply designing replacements for traditional craft methods; they were inventing tools that were capable of previously unimagined accuracy. Moreover, these were also extremely skilled craftsmen. Indeed, the ability to actually make—with their own hands—what they conceived is an integral part of their achievements. "It is one thing to invent," observed Marc Brunel, "and another thing to make the invention work."[2]

An affinity for steel and iron is a gift, like perfect pitch for a musician. These engineers had the artist's independence. Joseph Clement once received an order from America for a large regulating screw to be made "in the best possible manner." He produced an object of unparalleled accuracy and submitted a bill for several hundred pounds to his shocked client, who had expected to pay at most twenty (the case went before arbitrators and the American lost). In another case, Isambard Kingdom Brunel, who was in charge of building the Great Western Railway, commissioned Clement to design a piercing locomotive whistle. Delighted with the prototype, Brunel ordered a hundred. He, too, was shocked at the high price and declared that it was six times what he had previously been paying. "That may be," responded Clement, "but mine are more than six times better. You ordered a first-rate article, and you must be content to pay for it."[3] He won that case, too.

Mechanical genius is less well understood and studied than artistic genius, yet it surely is analogous. "Is not invention the poetry of science?" asked E. M. Bataille, a French pioneer of the steam engine. "All great discoveries carry with them the indelible mark of poetic thought. It is necessary to be a poet to create."[4] Nevertheless, while most of us would bridle at the suggestion that if Cézanne, say, had not lived, someone else would have created similar paintings, we readily accept the notion that the emergence of a new technology is inevitable or, at least, determined by necessity. My search for the best tool of the millennium suggests otherwise. Some tools were developed in direct response to a particularly vexing problem—this was the case with the Roman frame saw, or the socketed hammer. No doubt these devices would have appeared sooner or later. But the sudden and "mysterious" appearance of tools such as the carpenter's brace or the medieval bench lathe cannot be explained by necessity. Such tools are the result of leaps of an individual's creative imagination. They are the product of brilliant, inventive minds whose intuitive perceptions of complex mechanical relationships really are poetic.

The screwdriver is hardly poetic. The pragmatic way in which the arquebusier's spanner and the armorer's pincers were modified to include a screwdriver, or the casual combination of a screwdriver bit with a carpenter's brace, suggest expediency rather than invention. The screw itself, however, is a different matter. It is hard to imagine that even an inspired gunsmith or armorer—let alone a village blacksmith—simply happened on the screw by accident. To begin with, the thread of a screw describes a particularly complicated three-dimensional shape, often misnamed a spiral. In fact, a spiral is a curve that winds around a fixed point with a continuously increasing radius. A clock spring forms a spiral; so does a rope neatly coiled on the deck of a sailing ship. A helix, on the other hand, is a three-dimensional curve that twists around a cylinder at a constant inclined angle.

So-called spiral staircases and spiral bindings are both examples of helixes. So, of course, are screws.

The helix occurs in nature in the form of the climbing vine and in some seashells.* But it requires a particular set of talents to invent a screw. First, it would take a skillful mathematician to describe the geometry of the helix. Then he—or someone else—would have to make the connection between theoretical mathematics and practical mechanics in order to imagine a use for such an unusual object. Finally, there would be the problem of how to actually fabricate a screw.

The builder of the *Housebook* lathe, whoever he was, resolved the problem of how to make a screw, but he did not invent the screw itself. An understanding of the principle of the screw predates the fifteenth century. The first documented use of the word *screw*, according to the *Oxford English Dictionary*, is in 1404. It occurs in a list of accounts: "Item 1 rabitstoke cum 2 scrwes" (the word was also spelled *skrew, skrue,* and *scrue*). A rabitstoke, I learn, is a plane for shaping complicated grooves, or rabbits; the two wooden screws, holding an adjustable fence, are part of the tool.[5] Small wooden screws were also used to make bench vises and assorted

---

*The Latin for screw is *cochlea*, which is Greek for "snail" or "snail shell." The Latin for vine is *vitis*, which is the root of the French word *vis*, or screw, whence the English *vise*.

clamps; large wooden screws adjusted the vertical and horizontal angle of cannons.

The most famous use of screws in the Middle Ages was in printing presses. Johannes Gutenberg played a pivotal role in the invention of movable type in the mid-1400s; unfortunately, there is no surviving description of his press. The earliest known representation of a printing press is about fifty years later. It consists of a heavy wood frame with a crosspiece through which a large screw is threaded. The screw is turned by means of a handspike, or lever, and pushes down a wooden board, which in turn presses the paper against the inked type.

The medieval printing press was likely an adaptation of a similar press that was used in paper-making. Stacks of damp sheets of paper, alternating with layers of felt cloth, were squeezed dry between two boards. But there might have been other models, for presses had many applications in medieval times. Linen presses, which were found in every large household, gave freshly woven cloth a smooth, lustrous finish. Olive and grape presses were used for pressing olive oil and wine. Apple presses made apple juice; seed presses squeezed oil from rapeseed and flax. All these presses used a vertical screw that was turned to exert downward pressure.

The printing press and the paper press were medieval devices, but linen presses had been used since Roman times. A picture of a linen press with a heavy

Printers at work, Frankfurt-am-Main, 1568.

wooden frame and not one but two screws survives in a Pompeian fresco. The origins of olive and wine presses are ancient, too. The Roman architect Marcus Vitruvius Pollio, who lived sometime in the first century B.C., mentions olive-oil presses in *The Ten Books on Architecture*. In a passage on farmhouse planning, he describes a "pressing room" where olives are pressed to make oil. He writes that the room should be not less than forty feet long in order to accommodate the traditional beam press, but adds that such a large room is not required if the press is worked by "turning screws."[6]

Medieval paper press.

The discovery of the screw press is described in detail in *Historia Naturalis*, published in A.D. 66 by Pliny the Elder. Pliny credits Hero of Alexandria with the invention. Hero was a mathematician (he discovered the formula for calculating the area of a triangle), but like most ancient mathematicians, he was also interested in mechanics. According to Pliny, Hero began his experiments with presses by improving the traditional beam press. The beam press consisted of a long wooden beam (*prelum*) whose end was inserted into a pocket in a wall. The beam was raised, and a bag of macerated olive pulp was placed beneath it, like a nut in a giant nutcracker. Then the beam was pulled down by means of a rope wound around a drum. To get rid of the clumsy rope, Hero inserted a large wooden screw, fixed to floor and

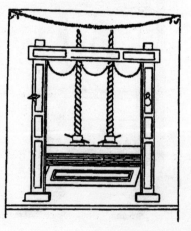

Roman linen press, from a mural painting found in Pompeii.

ceiling, through the beam. As a nut was turned, the beam was forced down. This worked well, but Hero found that the nut had a tendency to jam. He then took a different tack. He attached a heavy stone to the bottom of the screw. Now, as the screw was turned, it lifted the stone, whose weight carried the beam down. "When you have hung up the stone and left it to itself," Hero wrote, "the *prelum* will do the pressing without your having to repeat the pressure several times."[7]

Pliny describes the weighted beam press as "very much praised." Nevertheless, pulling *up* a weight in order to pull *down* a beam is hardly elegant, and Hero was not satisfied. Instead of pulling a weight up, he asked himself, what if the screw was used to push down? At the same time, what if the *prelum* was eliminated altogether? Thus Hero invented the direct-screw press, the ancestor of the printing press. In fact, his machine is virtually indistinguishable from later presses. "We fix on the table two uprights," Hero writes in his detailed and lucid description, "which carry the crosspiece. . . . The screw hole should be in the middle of the crosspiece. The screw is put through this hole and turned by means of handspikes till it reaches the lid which is laid on the *galeagra* [the box containing the fruit] and presses it down and the juice flows."*[8]

---

*The technology of olive and grape presses was identical.

The screw-down press is a marvelous invention, not only because it is simple and compact but also because it is capable of enormous pressure. The downward force is a direct function of the ratio between the pitch of the screw and the circumference described by the handspike. For example, imagine a press of the type described by Hero whose large screw has a pitch of one inch, and which is turned by means of a handspike three feet long. If a man applies a force of, say, forty pounds to the handspike, the pressure exerted on the olive pulp will be more than nine *thousand* pounds. The ability of a single man— working without animals or waterpower—to exert this kind of force was unprecedented.

Hero invented a variety of machines in which he often incorporated a common mechanical device that the ancient Greeks called an "endless screw," today referred

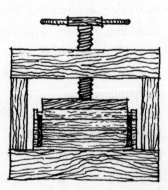

Hero's direct-screw press.

to as a worm gear. A worm gear is a combination of a long screw and a toothed wheel; each revolution of the screw advances the wheel a minute distance. The mechanical advantage depends on the pitch of the screw and the number of teeth in the wheel. Hero incorporated several endless screws into his hodometer, or "road measurer." The instrument was fixed atop a cart whose axle powered a train of endless screws that, at predetermined intervals, released a pebble into a box. The surveyor had only to count the pebbles to compute the distance traversed. Hero also invented the *dioptra*, an ancestor of the theodolite. The *dioptra* was mounted on a tripod or pedestal and the surveyor squinted down a sight whose horizontal and vertical orientation he adjusted by means of two worm gears, here used as regulating screws.

The screws used in ancient worm gears were usually bronze; screws for presses were wood. Both screws were made by tracing a helix onto a cylinder or rod and filing or carving the thread by hand. The template was a sheet of soft metal in the shape of a right-angled triangle. According to the ancient instructions, the triangle was wrapped around the rod so that one arm of the right angle was parallel to the axis, the hypotenuse automatically tracing a helix on the rod.[9] I couldn't quite imagine this, so I thought I would try it using a piece of triangular paper and a broomstick handle. When I finished

A worm gear.

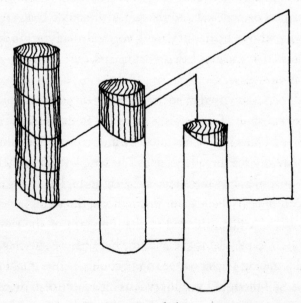

Tracing a helix.

wrapping the triangular piece of paper around the stick, indeed, the edge of the paper made a neat helix. The problem was that there was no way to trace it without cutting through the paper. The instructions clearly stated that the template was reused. I realized that my mistake was to start wrapping with the vertical of the triangle against the broomstick. If I started with the point of the triangle, I could trace the hypotenuse, section by section, as I unwrapped the paper.

Another Greek device that used screws was called a "tortoise." The tortoise was a primitive nut made of a block of wood, drilled with a smooth hole, inside which was an iron or copper peg, called a *tylos*. The screw went into the hole, and as the *tylos* engaged the rotating thread, the tortoise "crawled" along the rotating screw. The tortoise is said to have originated in an apparatus for resetting fractured bones and is attributed to Andreas, a physician who lived in the third century B.C. This machine, which has an unfortunate resemblance to the torturer's rack, used the tortoise to gradually pull a harness that stretched the fractured limb. The tortoise was also used in adjustable obstetric instruments such as clamps and dilators.[10]

Since the friction between the *tylos* and the threads of the screw was too great to allow much force to be exerted, the tortoise could be used only with relatively small devices. The massive screw of Hero's beam press would have jammed if he had used a *tylos*. He needed a different way of engaging the screw. Pondering the problem, Hero made another momentous discovery: the (male) screw has a (female) counterpart: the nut. We do not know exactly how he made this breakthrough. Perhaps he tried several pegs and intuited a continuous female thread. Maybe he thought it through mathematically. Or did it come in a flash of inspiration? Once he had the idea. It was a relatively simple matter to make a nut: using a Roman auger, he drilled a hole in a block of wood, split it in two, carved the female threads, and put the parts back together.

When it came to the screw-down press, however, Hero had to find a way to cut the threads inside a hole, leaving the heavy cross-beam intact. This was a challenge, but Hero was undeterred. He invented what is, as

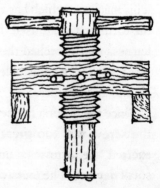

Hero's screw tap.

far as we know, the world's first screw tap. It was a box containing a wooden lead screw, guided by several *tylos*. The tip of the lead screw was fitted with an iron cutter. With the box firmly attached to the piece of wood in which a hole had been drilled, the lead screw was turned, and the cutter descended into the hole. "And we turn it till it comes into the plank, and we keep on turning it up and down, and we serve the wedge with blows again and again, until we have cut out the female screw with the furrow we wanted," instructed Hero. "And so we have made the female screw."[11] In 1932, a Danish historian, Aage Gerhardt Drachmann, made a drawing of the screw tap from Hero's detailed written description. When a colleague challenged the practicability of the device and declared it "technically impossible," the intrepid Dane built a working model and successfully threaded a two-inch hole in a beechwood plank.[12]

There is textual evidence that the Romans used screw taps with iron as well as wood. Josephus, a Jewish historian who lived in the first century A.D., writes of the temple in Jerusalem and describes eight-and-a-half-foot-long iron tie-rods that reinforced the supporting columns. "The head of each rod passed into the next by means of a cleverly made socket crafted in the form of a screw." Later, he elaborates: "They were held by these sockets, the male fitting into the female."[13] These female sockets must have been threaded. Pappus of Alexandria, one of the last great Greek mathematicians, who lived in the fourth century, writes that "a screw is constructed having a helix with oblique threads in the drum made to fit in with *another* [emphasis added]," which might be a nut and bolt.[14] Vitruvius is clearer. In describing a *trispast*, a crane that looked like a wooden A-frame, he writes that the two timbers "are fastened together at the upper end by a bolt."[15] Oddly, archaeological evidence for nuts and bolts is extremely slim. Indeed, there is only one surviving Roman nut. Displayed in the Provincial Museum of Bonn, it is wrought iron, approximately one and a quarter inches square with a half-inch-diameter threaded hole. The nut was discovered in the 1890s among Roman relics dated A.D. 180–260 on the site of a fortified camp in Germany.[16] No bolt was found.

If nuts and bolts were used only to assemble demountable structures such as the crane described by Vitruvius, that may explain why so few have been found. One thing is certain, the Romans—despite being skilled ironworkers and having invented nails—never made the connection between bolts and screws. Roman screws and screwdrivers are nowhere written about, and none have been discovered. "Necessity is the mother of invention" is an old Roman saying. Of course, the Romans had neither matchlocks nor butt hinges, so perhaps they felt no pressing need to develop a small, effective fastener. On the other hand, they did use bellows, and as

Agricola pointed out, screws were superior to nails. Yet there is no such thing as a technological imperative. It would take another fourteen hundred years for the screw to appear. That is, it would take another fourteen hundred years for a mechanical poet to realize that the helix that could press olives, stretch broken limbs, and adjust surveying instruments could also serve as a kind of threaded nail.

CHAPTER SEVEN

Father of the Screw

HERO OF ALEXANDRIA was a Greek. I had been taught that mechanical expertise was the preserve of the Romans, who invented the arch and the dome, never mind the auger and the plane. The Greeks were philosophers and artists. As a student, I had been to Greece, climbed the Acropolis, and visited museums. But, like many people, I had misinterpreted what I had seen. "So little has come down to us from the Greek Miracle, decisive for the birth of our sort of civilization, that we have become used to making a great deal of the things we have," wrote Derek J. de Solla Price, a Yale professor of the history of science. "Preservation has been highly selective so that we tend to see the Greeks in terms of only the more indestructible masses of building stone, statuary, and ceramic together with coins and a few grave goods that are the main holdings of our museums and archaeological sites."[1] Indeed, the material evidence for Greek mechanical devices is so scant that, according to Price, it was long thought that the Greeks simply did not use complex machines, and that the surviving written descriptions of machines, by authors such as Hero, were merely speculative.

This belief was altered by a momentous discovery. Like many archaeological finds, it came about largely by chance. In 1900, two boats belonging to sponge fishermen were crossing the strait that lies between Crete and the Greek mainland and were swept off course by a squall. They sought shelter in the lee of an uninhabited islet called Antikythera. When the storm abated, the divers explored the unfamiliar waters, looking for sponges. Instead, at a depth of 140 feet, they discovered the remains of an ancient ship surrounded by scattered bronze and marble statues. They reported their find to the authorities, who organized an archaeological expedition.

The pottery dated the shipwreck between 80 and 50 B.C. The vessel appeared to have been a trader, sailing from somewhere in Asia Minor—perhaps the island of Rhodes—and bound for Rome. The salvaged material included many fragments encrusted with two thousand years of debris. The fragments were set aside while the archaeologists turned their attention to restoring the statues. Occasionally, the restorers went through the debris hoping to locate a missing piece of statue. Eight months into the work, during one such search, they made a startling discovery. One of the encrusted lumps had split apart, probably as the ancient wood inside shrank after being exposed to the atmosphere. The break revealed not a piece of statue but several corroded and crumbling bronze disks with inscriptions, as well as the traces of what appeared to be gearwheels. The mechanical device, whatever it was, had been contained in a wooden case about eight inches high, six inches wide, and four inches thick.

Preliminary cleaning revealed that the so-called Antikythera Mechanism was a machine of great complexity with many interlocking gearwheels. However, the heavy calcareous accretions on the fragile corroded fragments, many of which were fused together, made accurate reconstruction difficult. Some archaeologists believed that it was an ancient astrolabe; others argued that it was too complicated to be a navigation device and had to be some sort of clock. Since the oldest evidence of geared clockwork in Muslim and Chinese astronomical machines was no earlier than about A.D. 1000, to many scholars it seemed outlandish to suggest that the Greeks had this technology a thousand years earlier.[2] Some argued that the mechanism was not ancient at all and had to be part of a later shipwreck on the same site. The last claim, at least, was laid to rest when it was ascertained that the disks were definitely bronze, a material used only in ancient times, more modern instruments being made of brass.

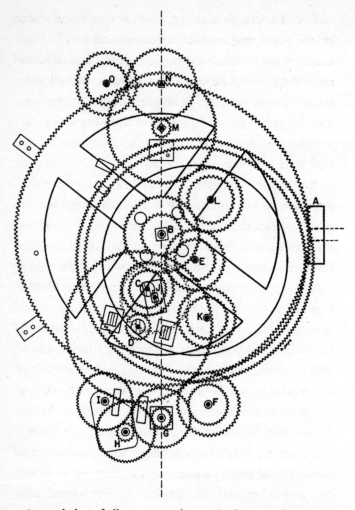

General plan of all gearing in the Antikythera Mechanism.

Decades later, as cleaning techniques improved, more of the inscriptions were deciphered and more of the mechanism was revealed. Yet the purpose of the machine remained a mystery. In 1959, Derek J. de Solla Price, who had been studying the Antikythera Mechanism, published a cover article in *Scientific American* titled "An Ancient Greek Computer." He speculated that the device was used to calculate the motion of stars and planets, which made it an ancient forebear of De'Dondi's planetary clock.[3] Since the first known mechanical clock dated from the fourteenth century, this again brought counterclaims that such sophisticated technology could not have belonged to the ancient Greeks, and that the mechanism must be of later vintage. In 1971, Price and his Greek colleagues began to examine the fragments using the then new technology of gamma-radiographs and x-radiographs. They discerned layers of the mechanism previously hidden within the encrusted fragments. The final part of the puzzle fell into place when a missing crucial piece was found in the museum storeroom. It was now possible to reconstruct the machine.

According to Price, "The mechanism is like a great astronomical clock without an escapement, or like a modern analogue computer which uses mechanical parts to save tedious calculation."[4] The front dial is inscribed with the signs of the zodiac, and a slip ring shows the months of the year; two back dials, one with three slip rings, one with four, indicate lunar and planetary phenomena. Inside, the movement consists of more than thirty interlocking toothed gearwheels assembled with pins and wedges—no screws. Most of these wheels are simple circular gears that transmit and modify rotary motion, the triangular teeth of one gear engaging the teeth of the other. Price also discovered a more complex set of gears that compound two different rates of revolution—the sidereal motions of the sun and the waxing and waning of the moon—to produce the cycles of the so-called synodic month. This is, in fact, the first known example of a differential gear. The differential in the axle of automobiles, which divides power between the driving wheels and allows the inside wheel to travel a shorter distance smoothly when the vehicle is turning a corner, was invented in 1827; the differential gear in the Antikythera Mechanism was made two thousand years ago. "It is a bit frightening to know that just before the fall of their great civilization the ancient Greeks had come so close to our age," writes Price, "not only in their thought, but also in their scientific technology."[5]

The Antikythera Mechanism is the only complex mechanical instrument to survive from antiquity, yet we know that it was not unique. A similar device is described by Cicero, who witnessed a demonstration of a "celestial globe" in the first century B.C. "When Gallus set this globe in motion, it came about that the moon was as many revolutions behind the sun on the bronze instrument as in the heavens themselves, and therefore there was that same eclipse of the sun in that sphere, and the moon then met that point, which is the earth's shadow." Cicero was impressed. "I decided then that there was more genius in that Sicilian than human nature seems able to encompass."[6] "That Sicilian" was Archimedes, the builder of the celestial globe, who had died about one hundred and fifty years earlier. Archimedes' globe was famous in the ancient world; it is also referred to by Plutarch and Ovid. Even eight hundred years after Archimedes' death, Claudianus wrote a poem in which Jupiter was mocked by the "skill of an old man of Syracuse [who] has copied the laws of the heavens, nature's reliability, and the ordinances of the gods."[7] None of these authors provided technical details, however. We know from ancient references that Archimedes himself wrote a treatise titled *On Sphere-Making*, but it has long been lost. Price speculates that Archimedes probably used a complicated gear train of the type found in the Antikythera Mechanism, which appears to be a later copy of his celestial globe.

Archimedes was a citizen of Syracuse, a wealthy Greek city-state on the island of Sicily. He was born about 287 B.C., the son of an astronomer, and was sent as a young man to study mathematics in Alexandria with the successors of the great Euclid. On his return to

Syracuse, he devoted himself to science. He became the foremost mathematician of the ancient world, devising a variety of proofs in both plane and solid geometry, including describing the geometry of the spiral. He wrote several treatises on the equilibrium of planes and established the mathematical foundation for the science of mechanics. In addition, he single-handedly invented the science of hydrostatics, the branch of physics that deals with fluids at rest and under pressure.

Archimedes left instructions that his sepulchral column include a depiction of his favorite proposition: the calculation of the exact ratio between a sphere and the cylinder that circumscribed it. He died at the age of seventy-five. One hundred and fifty years later, Cicero, while serving as Roman administrator of Sicily, sought out the tomb and, finding it neglected, had it restored. Cicero anticipated the interest in Archimedes by later historians such as Diodorus Siculus, Livy, and Plutarch. Of course, they wrote three hundred years (in the case of Plutarch, four hundred years) after the fact; by then, all that was left were stories. One of these concerned Archimedes' death. During the Second Punic War, Syracuse was attacked by the Roman army, and after a two-year siege the city fell. According to Plutarch, the victorious Roman general, Marcellus, who was an amateur mathematician, sent a soldier to fetch the renowned Archimedes. "As fate would have it, he [Archimedes] was intent on working out some problem with a diagram, and having fixed his mind and his eyes alike on his investigation, he never noticed the incursion of the Romans nor the capture of the city," Plutarch writes. "And when a soldier came up to him suddenly and bade him follow to Marcellus, he refused to do so until he had worked out his problem to a demonstration; whereat the soldier was so enraged that he drew his sword and slew him."[8] The remorseful Marcellus is said to have personally erected the mathematician's tomb. He also appropriated two of Archimedes' celestial globes, one of which later came into the hands of the astronomer Gallus, who showed it to Cicero.

The most famous story told about Archimedes concerns his solution of the so-called wreath problem. Hieron, the king of Syracuse, commissioned a gold wreath as an offering to the gods. He provided gold to the jeweler, who in due time delivered the finished wreath. Hieron suspected that the gold had been diluted with silver, but could not prove it. The wreath was a consecrated object and could not be tampered with, so a chemical assay was out of the question. Since the goldsmith refused to confess, the king turned to Archimedes. The mathematician pondered the matter and devised a simple experiment. He weighed the wreath, and immersed similar weights of silver and gold in a vessel of water, measuring how much water each displaced. He discovered that silver displaces more water than gold (the specific gravity of silver is almost half that of gold). Since the immersed wreath caused more water to overflow than the equivalent weight of gold, he deduced the presence of silver and proved that the wreath was indeed impure. According to legend, the idea for the water experiment came to Archimedes as he was plunging himself into a tub in a public bath. Seeing the water overflowing triggered something in his mind. "Transported with joy, he jumped out of the tub and rushed home naked," writes Vitruvius, "crying out in a loud voice, 'Heurēka! Heurēka!' [I've found it! I've found it!]."[9]

Plutarch wrote that Archimedes "regarded as sordid and ignoble the construction of instruments, and in general every art directed to use and profit, and he only strove after those things which, in their beauty and excellence, remain beyond all contact with the common needs of life."[10] Yet there is no doubt that the mathematician had a mechanical bent, no less than Hero or Maudslay. Archimedes' reputation for cleverness and ingenuity was legendary. The Romans named a popular puzzle, which consisted of various-shaped pieces of ivory that had to be assembled into a square, *Loculus Archimedius* in his honor. His cleverness manifested itself in many practical inventions, all still in use: the compound pulley, whose several sheaves increased lifting power and allowed a single man to raise heavy weights; the windlass, a rope wound around a drum, which was used as a hoisting device aboard ships and in mines; and the ancestor of the balancing weighing scale, the steelyard. In addition to the celestial globe, he is said to have built a water clock and a hydraulic organ in which air was compressed by water.

Like Leonardo and Ramelli, Archimedes served as a military engineer. During the siege of Syracuse he was called on to build defensive weapons. He designed catapults that threw rocks weighing five hundred pounds, and complicated underwater obstacles that capsized ships. His most renowned weapon was a mirror that beamed the sun's rays and set the attackers' ships on fire. To prove the practicality of what had long been considered merely a colorful legend, in 1973, a Greek engineer named Ioannis Sakas built a working version of the ancient ray gun.[11] He used seventy bronze-coated mirrors, which he aimed at a tarred plywood cutout of a ship. At a distance of 165 feet, approximating the "bowshot" that is mentioned in the classical text, it took only a few minutes for fire to break out.

In 1981, the redoubtable Sakas tested another Archimedean invention, the *architronito*, or steam cannon. This device was credited to Archimedes by Leonardo da Vinci, whose sketchbooks show a gun barrel with a breech encased in a heated firebox. When water is released from a cistern into the white-hot barrel, the resulting steam creates sufficient pressure to eject the cannonball. Leonardo wrote that "this machine has driven a ball weighing one talent [about twenty pounds] six stadia [about three thousand feet]."[12] Sakas's scale model successfully fired a cement-filled tennis ball a distance of two hundred feet.[13]

According to Plutarch, after Archimedes had written a treatise titled "To Move a Given Weight by a Given Force," in which he claimed that any weight could be moved, Hieron challenged the mathematician to prove his assertion by moving a beached ship loaded with freight. Archimedes set up his apparatus, attached a line to the ship, "and then drew it along, smoothly and evenly as if it were floating in water, not with great labor, but sitting down at a distance."[14] It was on that occasion that he made his famous claim: "Just give me somewhere to stand, and I shall move the earth."[15] How could Archimedes move a vessel weighing as much as seventy-five tons? According to Plutarch, it was done with a compound pulley; a description by a Byzantine historian mentions a three-sheaved pulley; and Athenaeus, a Greek historian, writes that Archimedes used an endless screw. A. G. Drachmann suggested that it is not unreasonable to assume that the ship was moved by a combination of these machines. He calculated the mechanical advantage of a pulley of five sheaves, pulled by a windlass that was powered by a combination of endless screws, would be 1:125,000.[16] That is, one pound of force on the rope would translate into a pulling force of more than sixty tons. Even assuming losses for friction, Drachmann argued, Archimedes alone—the different versions are in agreement on this point—could easily move the heavy ship a small distance.

Who was the inventor of the endless screw? Some modern historians credit Archytas of Terentum, a Pythagorean philosopher who lived at the time of Plato, around 400 B.C.; others point to Apollonius of Perge, a younger contemporary of Archimedes'.[17] Drachmann champions Archimedes himself, citing not only Athenaeus' story of moving the ship, but also quoting Eustathius, a Greek scholar who wrote, "Screw is also the name of a sort of machine, which was first invented by Archimedes."[18]

Drachmann's claim is all the more plausible since Archimedes' name is associated with another kind of screw, the water screw, a device for lifting water. The water screw consists of a giant screw about one foot in diameter and ten to fifteen feet long, encased in a watertight wooden tube. The tube, whose ends are left open, is installed at a low angle, with the lower end immersed in water. As the entire apparatus turns, powered by a person walking on cleats fastened to the exterior, the water entering the lower end is moved up by the helical partitions—or threads—of the screw and emerges at the top. The water screw turns slowly, but its capacity is substantial (the lower the angle, the greater the flow), and its mechanical efficiency has been estimated to be as much as 60 percent, which compares favorably with later water-lifting devices such as waterwheels and bucket conveyor belts.*[19]

The oldest references to the water screw, in the second century B.C., all credit Archimedes with the invention. According to Diodorus, Archimedes invented the water screw while he was a young man in Alexandria.[20] That makes sense. The device is ideal for agricultural irrigation in Egypt: unlike large waterwheels, it can easily be moved from place to place; its lift is not great, but sufficient for the flat delta; and the simple design— there are no moving parts—resists clogging by the silted Nile River water.

Water screw technology spread from Egypt throughout the Mediterranean. Water screws were used for irrigation, but they had other applications. Archimedes is said to have used them to empty bilge water from one of Hieron's huge ships. Water screws were also used by the Romans to lift water in municipal water systems, and to pump out mines. Several well-preserved wooden water

---

*The Archimedean screw continues in use to this day. In modern screw-conveyors, the screw rotates inside the cylinder; in the ancient version, the entire cylinder rotated.

screws were discovered in the early 1900s in ancient Roman copper mines in Spain.[21] The twelve-foot-long tubes, approximately one foot in diameter, are wrapped in pitched cloth and strengthened with rope; inside, the helical partitions are made of laminated strips of wood, glued and attached with copper nails. Four such water screws in series could lift water a vertical distance of about twenty feet. Diodorus describes how "with constant pumping by turns they throw up the water to the mouth of the pit and thus drain the mine; for this engine is so ingeniously contrived that a vast quantity of water is strangely and with little labor cast out."[22]

Diodorus was impressed with the simplicity and effectiveness of the water screw since he compared it to other ancient water-lifting devices such as complicated bucket conveyor belts and waterwheels. A common type of waterwheel was the *tympanum,* a large hollow wheel, ten

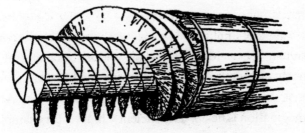

Archimedean screw, from a later edition of Vitruvius, *The Ten Books on Architecture,* first century B.C.

to fifteen feet in diameter, divided into eight pie-shaped compartments. As the wheel turned, water flowed into the lowest compartment when it was submerged, and out when the compartment reached the top position. It has been suggested that the *tympanum* may have inspired Archimedes.[23] Indeed, if the *tympanum* shape is stretched and rotated along its central axis, it produces a cylindrical helix. This three-dimensional extrapolation, although hardly obvious, would not have been difficult for a skilled mathematician. The presumed authorship of Archimedes is supported by another curious fact. The only detailed description of a water screw in all Greek and Latin literature, which is by Vitruvius, specifies a water screw with *eight* helical partitions—the precise number that would be produced if the water screw were inspired by the *tympanum*.[24] Vitruvius was presumably describing the original water screw; later Roman engineers, realizing that there is no mechanical advantage to eight partitions—and considerable added cost—reduced their number to two or three.

Whether or not Archimedes was inspired by the *tympanum*, the water screw is yet another example of a mechanical invention that owes its existence to human imagination rather than technological evolution. And imagination is fickle. The ancient Chinese, for example, did not know the water screw; indeed, they didn't know screws at all: the screw is the only major mechanical device that they did not independently invent.[25] The Romans, on the other hand, knew about the screw when they invented the auger, yet they never realized that the same principle could solve a major drilling problem: the tendency of deep holes to become clogged with sawdust. Not until the early 1800s was the so-called spiral auger, whose helical shank cleared the sawdust as the bit turned, invented.

The water screw is not only a simple and ingenious machine, it is also, as far as we know, the first appearance in human history of the helix. The discovery of the screw represents a kind of miracle. Only a mathematical genius like Archimedes could have described the geometry of the helix in the first place, and only a mechanical genius like him could have conceived a practical application for this unusual shape. If he invented the water screw as a young man in Alexandria, and—as I like to think—later adapted the idea of the helix to the endless screw, then we must add a small but hardly trifling honor to his many distinguished achievements: Father of the Screw.

GLOSSARY OF TOOLS

*Undertaker's
screwdriver*

*Gent's
fancy
screwdriver*

*London
pattern
screwdriver*

*Scotch
pattern
screwdriver*

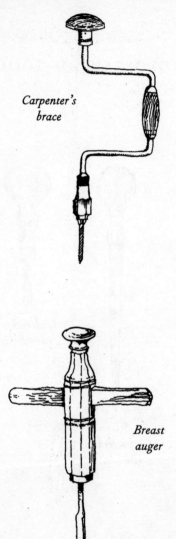

*Carpenter's
brace*

*Breast
auger*

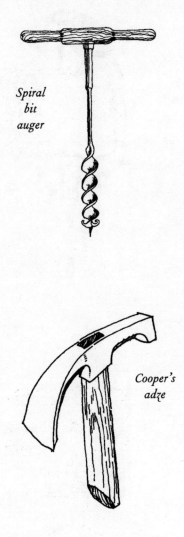

*Spiral
bit
auger*

*Cooper's
adze*

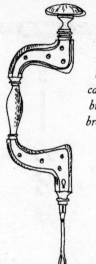

Wooden carpenter's brace with brass plates

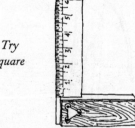

Try square

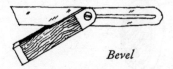

Bevel

A-level

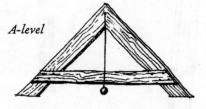

Spirit level

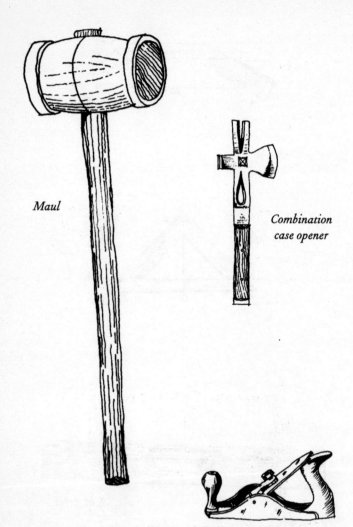

Maul

Combination
case opener

Plane

Backsaw

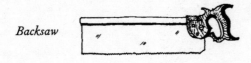

Skew-back handsaw

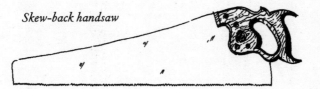

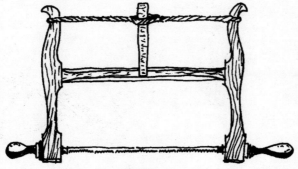

Frame saw

ACKNOWLEDGMENTS

Thanks, first, to David Shipley for asking the question. For help with the Greek quote, my appreciation to Prof. Ralph Rosen, chair of classical studies at the University of Pennsylvania. Robert A. Ruhloff was kind enough to send me information on wrought-iron spikes, including several interesting samples. Jamie Kendrick, Adam Barzilay, Maria Gonzalez, and Yi-Ting Liu provided capable research assistance. The Milton Historical Society supplied information on the redoubtable P. L. Robertson. The staff of the Fisher Fine Arts Library and the Van Pelt Library of the University of Pennsylvania were helpful, as always. I doubt that this small book would have seen the light of day without the encouragement of my editor, Nan Graham, and my agent, Carl Brandt, who both share my interest in tools and handy-work. Shirley Hallam, my wife, pointed me in the right direction, at the right time—as usual.

The Icehouse, Chestnut Hill, Pennsylvania

October 1999

NOTES

Chapter One: *The Carpenter's Toolbox*

1. Edward Rosen, "The Invention of Eyeglasses: Part I," *Journal of the History of Medicine* (January 1956): 34–35.

2. Ken Kern, *The Owner-Built Home* (Oakhurst, Calif.: Owner-Builder Publications, 1972), 78.

3. W. L. Goodman, *The History of Woodworking Tools* (London: G. Bell & Sons, 1964), 199–201.

4. R. A. Salaman, *Dictionary of Tools: used in the woodworking and allied trades, c. 1700–1970* (London: George Allen & Unwin Ltd., 1975), 299.

5. Lynn White Jr., "Technology and Invention in the Middle Ages," *Speculum* 15 (April 1940): 153.

6. For a dissenting view, see A. G. Drachmann, "The Crank in Graeco-Roman Antiquity," *Changing Perspectives in the History of Science: Essays in Honour of Joseph Needham* (London: Heinemann, 1973), 33–51.

7. Bertrand Gille, "Machines," in Charles Joseph Singer et al., eds., *A History of Technology: Vol. II, The Mediterranean Civilizations and the Middle Ages c. 700 B.C. to c. A.D. 1500* (New York: Oxford University Press, 1957), 651.

8. Bertrand Gille, "The Fifteenth and Sixteenth Centuries in the Western World," in Maurice Dumas, ed., *A History of Technology & Invention: Vol. II, The First Stages of Mechanization,*

trans. Eileen B. Hennessy (New York: Crown Publishers, 1969), 23.

9. Graham Hollister-Short, "Cranks and Scholars," *History of Technology* 17 (1995): 223–24.

10. Goodman, *History of Woodworking Tools*, 178.

11. Ibid., 9.

12. "Tools: Later development of hand tools: SCREW-BASED TOOLS: Screwdrivers and wrenches," *Britannica Online*, December 1998.

Chapter Two: *Turnscrews*

1. Peter Nicholson, *Mechanical Exercises: or, the elements and practice of Carpentry, Joinery, Bricklaying, Masonry, Slating, Plastering, Painting, Smithing, and Turning* (London: J. Taylor, 1812), 353.

2. Joseph Moxon, *Mechanick Exercises: or, the Doctrine of Handy-Works* (London: J. Moxon, 1693), A5–6.

3. *The Greek Anthology*, trans. W. R. Patton (London: William Heinemann, 1916), 405.

4. "Navigation," *Encyclopaedia Britannica*, vol. 12 (Edinburgh: A. Bell and C. Macfarquhar, 1797), plate 343. The reference is pointed out by Joseph E. Sandford, "Carpenters' Tool Notes," in Henry C. Mercer, *Ancient Carpenters' Tools: Together with Lumbermen's, Joiners' and Cabinet Makers' Tools in Use in the Eighteenth Century* (Doylestown, Pa.: Bucks County Historical Society, 1975), 311.

5. *A Dictionary of American English: on historical principles*, vol. 4 (Chicago: University of Chicago Press, 1944), 2045.

6. R. A. Salaman, *Dictionary of Tools: used in the woodworking and allied trades, c. 1700–1970* (London: George Allen & Unwin Ltd., 1975), 450.

7. Ibid., 449.

8. A. J. Roubo, "L'Art du Menuisier en Meubles," *Description des*

Arts et Métiers, vol. 19 (Paris: Académie des Sciences, 1772), 944 (author's translation).

9. *Encyclopédie: ou dictionnaire raisonné des sciences, des arts et des métiers,* vol. 17 (Neuchastel: Samuel Faulche & Co., 1765), 484 (author's translation).

10. Adolphe Hatzfeld and Arsène Darmesteter, *Dictionnaire Général de la Langue Française: du commencement du XVIIe siècle jusqu'à nos jours,* vol. 2 (Paris: Librairie Delagrave, 1932), 2171.

11. James M. Gaynor and Nancy L. Hagedorn, *Tools: Working Wood in Eighteenth-Century America* (Williamsburg, Va.: Colonial Williamsburg Foundation), 11.

12. Linda F. Dyke, *Henry Chapman Mercer: An Annotated Chronology* (Doylestown, Pa.: Bucks County Historical Society, 1989), 11.

13. Kenneth D. Roberts, *Some 19th Century English Woodworking Tools: Edge & Joiner Tools and Bit Braces* (Fitzwilliam, N.H.: Ken Roberts Publishing Co., 1980).

14. See Witold Rybczynski, "One Good Turn," *New York Times Magazine,* April 18, 1999, 133.

Chapter Three: *Lock, Stock, and Barrel*

1. Lynn White Jr., "The Act of Invention: Causes, Contexts, Continuities, and Consequences," *Technology and Culture* 3 (fall 1963): 486–500.

2. Martha Teach Gnudi, "Agostino Ramelli and Ambrose Bachot," *Technology and Culture* 15, no. 4 (October 1974): 619.

3. *The Various and Ingenious Machines of Agostino Ramelli (1588),* trans. Martha Teach Gnudi (Baltimore: Johns Hopkins University Press, 1976), 508.

4. Bert S. Hall, "A Revolving Bookcase by Agostino Ramelli," *Technology and Culture* 11, no. 4 (July 1970): 397.

5. Georgius Agricola, *De Re Metallica,* trans. H. C. Hoover and L. H. Hoover (New York: Dover Publications, 1950), 364.

6. Christoph Graf zu Waldburg Wolfegg, *Venus and Mars: The*

World of the Medieval Housebook (Munich: Prestel-Verlag, 1998), 8.

7. Hugh B. C. Pollard, *Pollard's History of Firearms*, Claude Blair, ed. (New York: Macmillan, 1983), 29.

8. John Keegan, *A History of Warfare* (New York: Alfred A. Knopf, 1993), 329.

9. Fernand Braudel, *The Structures of Everyday Life: Vol. I, The Limits of the Possible*, trans. Siân Reynolds (New York: Harper & Row, 1981), 392.

10. Pollard, *Pollard's History of Firearms*, 55.

11. Ibid., 35.

12. Ibid., 18.

13. Joseph Moxon, *Mechanick Exercises: or, the Doctrine of Handy-Works* (London: J. Moxon, 1693), 33–34.

14. Charles John Ffoulkes, *The Armourer and His Craft: From the XIth to the XVIth Century* (New York: Benjamin Blom, 1967), 55.

15. Claude Blair, *European Armour: circa 1066 to circa 1700* (London: B. T. Batsford Ltd., 1958), 162.

16. Ffoulkes, *Armourer and His Craft*, 24.

17. Ibid., plate V.

Chapter Four: *The Biggest Little Invention*

1. Georgius Agricola, *De Re Metallica*, trans. H. C. Hoover and L. H. Hoover (New York: Dover Publications, 1950), 364.

2. G. H. Baillie, C. Clutton, and C. A. Ilbert, *Britten's Old Clocks and Watches and Their Makers* (New York: E. P. Dutton, 1956), 14.

3. Ibid., 64.

4. Joseph Chamberlain, "Manufacture of Iron Wood Screws," in British Association for the Advancement of Science, Committee on Local Industries, *The Resources, Products, and Industrial History of Birmingham and the Midland Hardware District* (London: R. Hardwicke, 1866), 605–6.

5. Henry C. Mercer, *Ancient Carpenters' Tools: Together with Lum-*

bermen's, Joiners' and Cabinet Makers' Tools in Use in the Eigh-teenth Century (Doylestown, Pa.: Bucks County Historical Society, 1975), 259.

6. Quoted by H. W. Dickinson, "Origin and Manufacture of Wood Screws," *Transactions of the Newcomen Society* 22 (1941–42): 80.

7. Ibid., 81.

8. Ibid., 89.

9. Ken Lamb, *P.L.: Inventor of the Robertson Screw* (Milton, Ont.: Milton Historical Society, 1998), 35.

10. Ibid., 16.

11. Henry F. Phillips and Thomas M. Fitzpatrick, "Screw," U.S. patent number 2,046,839, July 7, 1936.

12. American Screw Company to Henry F. Phillips, March 27, 1933.

13. Mead Gliders, Chicago, to American Screw Company, April 26, 1938.

14. Wentling Woodcrafters, Camden, N.J., to American Screw Company, June 15, 1938.

15. "The Phillips Screw Company" (unpublished paper, Phillips Screw Company, Wakefield, Mass.).

16. *Consumer Reports* 60, no. 11 (November 1995): 695.

Chapter Five: *Delicate Adjustments*

1. L. T. C. Rolt, *A Short History of Machine Tools* (Cambridge, Mass.: MIT Press, 1965), 59.

2. Robert S. Woodbury, *Studies in the History of Machine Tools* (Cambridge, Mass.: MIT Press, 1972), 20–21.

3. Ibid., 49.

4. Christoph Graf zu Waldburg Wolfegg, *Venus and Mars: The World of the Medieval Housebook* (Munich: Prestel-Verlag, 1998), 88.

5. Jacques Besson, *Theatrum Machinarum* (Lyon: 1578), plate IX.

6. Charles Plumier, *L'art de tourner* (Lyon: 1701).

7. Maurice Daumas and André Garanger, "Industrial Mechanization," in *A History of Technology & Invention*, Maurice Daumas, ed., trans. Eileen B. Hennessy (New York: Crown Publishers, 1969), 271.

8. James Nasmyth, *James Nasmyth, Engineer: An Autobiography* (London: John Murray, 1885), 136.

9. Ibid., 144.

10. Ibid., 128.

11. L. T. C. Rolt, *Great Engineers* (London: G. Bell and Sons, 1962), 105.

12. Samuel Smiles, *Industrial Biography: Iron-Workers and Tool-Makers* (Boston: Ticknor & Fields, 1864), 282.

Chapter Six: *Mechanical Bent*

1. Samuel Smiles, *Industrial Biography: Iron-Workers and Tool-Makers* (Boston: Ticknor & Fields, 1864), 337.

2. Ibid., 223.

3. Ibid., 312.

4. Ibid., 204 (author's translation).

5. W. L. Goodman, *The History of Woodworking Tools* (London: G. Bell & Sons, 1964), 105.

6. Vitruvius, *The Ten Books on Architecture*, trans. Morris Hicky Morgan (New York: Dover Publications, 1960), 184.

7. A. G. Drachmann, "Ancient Oil Mills and Presses," *Kgl. Danske Videnskabernes Selskab, Archaeologisk-kunsthistoriske Meddelelser* 1, no.1 (1932): 73.

8. Ibid., 76.

9. Bertrand Gille, "Machines," in *A History of Technology*, vol. 2, Charles Joseph Singer et al., eds. (New York: Oxford University Press, 1957), 631–32.

10. John James Hall, "The Evolution of the Screw: Its Theory and Practical Application," *Horological Journal*, July 1929, 269–70.

11. Quoted in John W. Humphrey et al., *Greek and Roman Technology: A Sourcebook* (London: Routledge, 1998), 56.

12. A. G. Drachmann, "Heron's Screwcutter," *Journal of Hellenic Studies* 56 (1936): 72–77.

13. Quoted in Humphrey et al., *Greek and Roman Technology*, 56.

14. Quoted in Hall, "Evolution of the Screw: Its Theory and Practical Application," *Horological Journal*, August 1929: 285.

15. Vitruvius, *Ten Books*, 285.

16. Henry C. Mercer, *Ancient Carpenters' Tools: Together with Lumbermen's, Joiners' and Cabinet Makers' Tools in Use in the Eighteenth Century* (Doylestown, Pa.: Bucks County Historical Society, 1975), 273.

Chapter Seven: *Father of the Screw*

1. Derek J. de Solla Price, "Gears from the Greeks: The Antikythera Mechanism—a Calendar Computer from ca. 80 B.C.," *Transactions of the American Philosophical Society* 64, pt. 7 (November 1974): 51.

2. Derek J. de Solla Price, "Clockwork Before the Clock," *Horological Journal* (December 1955): 810–14.

3. Derek J. de Solla Price, "An Ancient Greek Computer," *Scientific American*, June 1959, 60–67.

4. Ibid., 66.

5. Ibid., 67.

6. Quoted in John W. Humphrey et al., *Greek and Roman Technology: A Sourcebook* (London: Routledge, 1998), 57–58.

7. Claudius Claudianus, *Shorter Poems* 51, in Humphrey et al., *Greek and Roman Technology*, 58.

8. Quoted in *The Works of Archimedes*, T. L. Heath, ed. (New York: Dover Publications, 1953), xviii.

9. Vitruvius, *The Ten Books on Architecture*, trans. Morris Hicky Morgan (New York: Dover Publications, 1960), 254.

10. Quoted in E. J. Dijksterhuis, *Archimedes*, trans. C. Dikshoorn (Copenhagen: Ejnar Munksgaard, 1956), 13.

11. *New York Times*, November 11, 1973.

12. Quoted in D. L. Simms, "Archimedes' Weapons of War and Leonardo," *British Journal of the History of Science* 21 (1988): 196.

13. *The Times*, May 15, 1981.

14. Quoted in A. G. Drachmann, "How Archimedes Expected to Move the Earth," *Centaurus* 5, no. 3–4 (1958): 278.

15. Quoted in Dijksterhuis, *Archimedes*, 15.

16. Drachmann, "How Archimedes Expected to Move the Earth," 280–81.

17. R. J. Forbes, "Hydraulic Engineering and Sanitation," *A History of Technology*, vol. 2, Charles Joseph Singer et al., eds. (New York: Oxford University Press, 1957), 677; A. G. Drachmann, *The Mechanical Technology of Greek and Roman Antiquity* (Copenhagen: Munksgaard, 1963), 204.

18. Quoted in A. G. Drachmann, "The Screw of Archimedes," *Actes de VIIIᵉ Congrès International d'Histoire des Sciences, Florence-Milan, 3–9 septembre 1956*, vol. 3 (Florence: Vinci, 1958), 940–41.

19. John Peter Oleson, *Greek and Roman Mechanical Water-Lifting Devices: The History of Technology* (Toronto: University of Toronto, 1984), 297, 365.

20. Humphrey et al., *Greek and Roman Technology*, 317.

21. William Giles Nash, *The Rio Tinto Mine: Its History and Romance* (London: Simpkin Marshall Hamilton Kent & Co., 1904), 35.

22. Diodorus Siculus, *The Historical Library of Diodorus the Sicilian; in Fifteen Books*, trans. G. Booth (London: W. M'Dowall for J. Davis, 1814).

23. See Drachmann, *Mechanical Technology*, 154.

24. Vitruvius, *Ten Books*, 297.

25. Joseph Needham and Wang Ling, *Science and Civilization in China, Introductory Orientations* (New York: Cambridge University Press, 1954), 241.

TEXT ILLUSTRATION SOURCES

Page 22: *A History of Technology: Vol. II, The Mediterranean Civilizations and the Middle Ages c. 700 B.C. to c. A.D. 1500*, eds. Charles Joseph Singer et al. (New York: Oxford University Press, 1956), 152; 42: Kenneth D. Roberts, *Some 19th Century English Woodworking Tools: Edge & Joiner Tools and Bit Braces* (Fitzwilliam, N.H.: Ken Roberts Publishing Co., 1980), 234; 50: *The Various and Ingenious Machines of Agostino Ramelli (1588)*, trans. Martha Teach Gnudi (Baltimore: Johns Hopkins University Press, 1976), plate 188; 52: *The Various and Ingenious Machines of Agostino Ramelli (1588)*, trans. Martha Teach Gnudi (Baltimore: Johns Hopkins University Press, 1976), plate 129; 58: *Wapenhandelinghe van Roers, Musquetten end Speissen, Achtervolgende de Ordre van Syn Excellente Maurits, Prince van Orangie . . . Figuirlyck vutgebeelt door Jacob de Gheyn* (Musket drill devised by Maurice of Orange) (The Hague, 1607); facsimile edition, New York: McGraw-Hill, 1971; 60: Hugh B. C. Pollard, *Pollard's History of Firearms*, ed. Claude Blair (New York: Macmillan, 1983), 35; 65: Charles John Ffoulkes, *The Armourer and His Craft: From the XIth to the XVIth Century* (New York: Benjamin Blom, 1967), 55. Redrawn by author; 66: Charles John Ffoulkes, *The Armourer and His Craft: From the XIth to the XVIth Century* (New York: Benjamin Blom, 1967), plate V. Redrawn by author; 80: Ken Lamb, *P.L.: Inventor of the Robertson Screw* (Milton, Ont.: Milton Historical Society, 1998), 152; 90: Christoph Graf zu Waldburg Wolfegg, *Venus and Mars: The World of the Medieval Housebook* (Munich: Prestel-Verlag,

1998), 88; 95: *A History of Technology: Vol. II, The Mediterranean Civilizations and the Middle Ages c. 700 B.C. to c. A.D. 1500*, eds. Charles Joseph Singer et al. (New York: Oxford University Press, 1956), 334; 98: Robert S. Woodbury, *Studies in the History of Machine Tools* (Cambridge, Mass.: MIT Press, 1972), Fig. 30; 114: T. K. Derry and Trevor I. Williams, *A Short History of Technology* (New York: Oxford University Press, 1960), 236; 118: A. G. Drachmann, *Ancient Oil Mills and Presses* (Copenhagen: Levin & Munksgaard, 1932), 159. Redrawn by author; 130: Derek J. de Solla Price, "Gears from the Greeks: The Antikythera Mechanism—a Calendar Computer from ca. 80 B.C.," *Transactions of the American Philosophical Society* 64, pt. 7 (November 1974): 37; 141: M. H. Morgan, Vitruvius, *The Ten Books on Architecture* (Cambridge, Mass.: Harvard University Press, 1946), 295. Pages 101, 115, 120, 122, 145–151 were drawn by the author.

INDEX

Witold Rybczynski is the author of nine books, including *Home: A Short History of an Idea*, *The Most Beautiful House in the World*, *Waiting for the Weekend*, *City Life*, and *A Clearing in the Distance*, for which he won The Christopher Award and the J. Anthony Lukas Prize. He is a regular contributor to *Atlantic Monthly*, *The New Yorker*, *The New York Times Magazine* and *The New York Review of Books*. He teaches at the University of Pennsylvania.